English Heritage

Book of
Roman Villas
and the Countryside

English ⌗ Heritage
Book of
Roman Villas
and the Countryside

Guy de la Bédoyère

B.T. Batsford Ltd / English Heritage
London

For H., T., R. and W.

Omnia explorate,
Meliora retinete

First published 1993

All rights reserved. No part of this publication
may be reproduced, in any form or by any means,
without permission from the Publisher.
Typeset by Goodfellow & Egan Phototypesetting
Ltd, Cambridge
and printed in Great Britain by
The Bath Press, Bath
Published by B.T. Batsford Ltd
4 Fitzhardinge Street, London W1H 0AH

A CIP catalogue record for this book is available
from the British Library

ISBN 0 7134 7045 3 (cased)
0 7134 7046 1 (limp)

Contents

Illustrations

Colour plates

Introduction

The landscape of modern England and Wales is scattered with the visible remains of the Romano-British countryside. Since early modern times the appearance of Roman antiquities in the ground has been noted. In 1658 the diarist and savant John Evelyn recorded: 'I found that digging about the bottom neere Sir Christopher Buckles neere Bansted [Banstead, Surrey] divers Medails have ben found both Coper and silver, with foundations of houses, urnes &c . . .'. By the late eighteenth and early nineteenth centuries knowledge of, and enthusiasm for, the classical world matched the neo-Classicism of the era. Samuel Lysons was one of the most well-known antiquarians of the day and he recorded in meticulous detail the mosaics uncovered at the Bignor (West Sussex) and Woodchester (Gloucestershire) villas (see **47** and **65**). Even Lullingstone's mosaic floor was briefly uncovered some time before 1788 during fencing work. In this case, though the floor was recognized for what it was, re-burial followed and the site was forgotten.

Of course the antiquarians had no detailed knowledge of the extent of Roman rural settlement, and tended to think only in terms of villas. Modern techniques, such as aerial photography have revealed that by far the majority, perhaps as much as ninety per cent, of the Romano-British population must have lived in the countryside. They lived in isolated small-holdings, small villages, or in one of the many houses which we call 'villas', ranging from modest comfortable houses to extravagantly appointed rural seats. Some lived in conditions scarcely distinguishable in the archaeological record from prehistoric times. Others enjoyed a sophisticated and comfortable standard of living. They were variously involved in agriculture, industry and leisure. Despite the hardships of living in the countryside in a pre-industrial landscape the rural Romano-British population did at least enjoy the advantages of the most effective infrastructure of trade and communications known in Britain until the coming of the turnpike roads and the canals in the eighteenth century.

Of course the countryside changed during the four centuries of the Roman period. When the Roman army arrived in AD 43 it found a native population dispersed among countless minor settlements. They were loosely divided into regional tribes which were led by chieftains at the head of a warrior aristocracy. The chieftains and their associates asserted themselves by pursuing territorial disputes, but for most of the rural population this would have hardly affected their day-to-day concerns about subsistence and the obligation to pay levies on their produce to whoever controlled their area at the time. In the south-east there were some signs of sophistication in the use of more advanced agricultural techniques imported from the continent of Europe. In the west and north, though, there had been little change for centuries, a feature carried on into the Roman period.

During the first two centuries of Roman rule the greatest changes took place in the towns. These had barely existed before but Roman provincial rule was operated through a structure of local government based on towns. Towns were often founded close to or on earlier native centres, retaining tribal identities. Enormous investments were made in urban infrastructure like public buildings and by the middle of the second century most of the *civitas* capitals and colonies enjoyed a range of facilities. Development in the countryside was by comparison slow. Although some exceptional houses of early date were built, like Fishbourne and Eccles, rural settlement seems to have benefited only gradually from the experience of being part of the Roman world.

During the third and fourth centuries, however, the position seems to have altered. Many rural villas developed into major estates and a number of small settlements that we might call villages emerged to take over some of the roles fulfilled by towns, while the towns themselves gradually diminished in importance. In many areas of southern Britain well-appointed houses are known to have existed in considerable numbers by the fourth century, sometimes only a mile or two apart. Conversely a number of native settlements in this area were abandoned by this time. There were also extensive areas in the south and in most of the north and far west where rural settlement remained much less sophisticated. Clearly there was an inequality in the Romano-British countryside.

It would be wrong to perceive the countryside as purely agricultural. Much would have remained as forest and there were also rural industries, the most conspicuous of which were the sprawling potteries of the upper Thames valley, and in and around the Alice Holt forest in Surrey. There were also livings to be made in the operation of rural shrines and temples, as centres of religious activity and relaxation and as sites for seasonal fairs and festivals. For the archaeologist this Romano-British rural community is represented by enormous numbers of sites of every category and the abundance of artefacts. By the fifth century the nature of the archaeological record was transformed – almost everything that we regard as helping to define a site as 'Roman' had virtually disappeared. The fate of the countryside is almost more enigmatic than the fate of the towns.

Despite the enormous changes in the landscape which have taken place since the turn of the century a surprising amount of the Roman countryside remains to this day. The most obvious survivals are the great villas like Ched-worth and Bignor, but there are also traces of native settlements in the west and north. Roman roads can be followed across great distances while in the Alice Holt forest the mounds that mark the sites of kilns can still be seen. Most modern archaeological studies are far less concerned with villas than they are with simpler farmsteads, native settlements, villages, land-use and the rural economy. Villas are being seen increasingly as nuclei of much larger economic units with tenants and workers all participating in production. As a result there is more interest in devising social and economic 'models' to explain how Romano-British society may have worked, and classifying different settlements. This work is very useful but in truth it is very rare that this kind of theorizing can be tied firmly to evidence, because the latter is so varied in its quality and distribution. This is a continual problem in a modern archaeology which seeks scientific and mathematical credibility but has to work with material which is rarely equal to the theoretical processes applied to it. So this book takes a historical point of view, tracing the development of the Roman countryside in all its aspects from its prehistoric origins right through to the post-Roman period. Where possible documented parallels from later periods have been referred to where they help shed light on the possible nature of life in rural Roman Britain.

I am grateful to Peter Kemmis Betty and Sarah Vernon-Hunt of Batsford, Stephen Johnson and Dr Anthony King for their help with the preparation of the text, and Catherine Johns of the British Museum for her help with some of the illustrations. I should thank my wife and children for their tolerance of my writing and also of numerous visits to sites and museums.

Drawings, paintings and photographs are by the author except those which have been kindly supplied by, and credited to, the British Museum and English Heritage. Where drawings are based on the work of others full acknowledgement has been made.

1 *Map of Roman Britain showing the principal rural sites, major towns and fortresses.*

1

The prehistoric countryside

Towards the end of the first century BC Britain stood at the edge of the Roman Empire. The tribal communities that occupied Britain had economies that were primarily agricultural. In other words most of the people were concerned for most of the time with the production of food. Any other production, for example that of pottery or metal goods, was limited in extent and is likely to have occupied only a very minor part of the effort expended in any one community. Not only were such activities likely to be seasonal or at best intermittent, but they would also have been suspended at times when food production was under strain. Every individual would have been directly affected daily by agricultural considerations. So the productive qualities of land dictated the distribution of peoples, provoked their territorial disputes and lay at the root of their spiritual concerns. The coming of Rome had a dramatic effect on the British tribes and created the curious hybrid which we call Romano-British society.

There are a number of literary sources which provide glimpses of this tribal world. They mainly supply tantalizing details of individuals engaged in power struggles; but they also contain enormously valuable references as to how the communities lived. There has always been a tendency to try and fit the archaeological evidence into this historical context. This is extremely difficult because the archaeological record will necessarily contain traces of events and movements which are not recorded in the surviving historical material. Similarly the historical material includes references to places which cannot easily be located today. But both forms of evidence are of great value and we need to review both in order to gain a broader picture of what life was like.

It would be wrong to perceive the late Iron Age countryside as a place where people continued to live as they had done for generations. We know from a growing body of evidence that agriculture was being improved and extended and that a surplus was being produced; this even included managing forests, rather than random tree-felling. Imported goods and coinage had become features of everyday life, at least for the better-off. The late Iron Age peoples of southern Britain in particular were close to the edge of an Empire which enjoyed many improvements in material goods and techniques. These filtered across the English Channel in various forms, whether as a result of migrating peoples or as a result of trade. The effect was that the prehistoric landscape of Britain was directly influenced and changed by the experience of being close to a much more developed society. Perhaps the best way of considering this situation is to look at how some Third World countries have experienced Western developments at arm's length. Equally the countryside exhibits a great degree of continuity into the Roman period and it is important to recognize this mix of tradition and innovation.

The historical evidence
Julius Caesar's abortive expeditions to Britain in 55 and 54 BC introduce us to the south-eastern part of Britain but only in terms which Caesar considered would interest his readers and elevate his status in Rome. He described Britain's inhabitants as being divided into the long-established indigenous peoples of the interior and the Belgic tribes of the south-east, the latter being relatively recent immigrants. The Belgic peoples he portrayed as comparatively civilized with a dense population engaged

in mixed agriculture and living in a large number of individual homesteads, whereas the indigenous peoples concentrated on pastoral farming.

Caesar creates the impression of a Britain where the degree of sophistication diminished as distance increased from the south-eastern corner. It is evident, though, that farming was well-established and he implies that the majority of the population lived and worked on individual farms. He adds supplementary information about the extraction of metals like tin and iron, and the use of a system of exchange based on coins and metal bars of fixed values.

A little more information comes from Strabo, a Greek geographer who was writing about the end of the first century BC. He noted that Britain produced cattle, corn, hides, dogs, silver, iron and slaves and that some of these were exported. He considered the Britons' knowledge of agricultural techniques to be poor and described temporary fortified settlements in forests.

The sequence of events in Caesar's campaigns need not concern us here but it is clear that the area which he explored contained a number of distinct tribal groups with their own identities and rulers. Among these rulers was one Cassivellaunus who ruled from somewhere north of the Thames. Caesar does not name Cassivellaunus' tribe but circumstantial references make it likely that he ruled the Catuvellauni, a tribe which dominated the area to the north of the Thames over the next century. Cassivellaunus held great sway over the other kings and was able to order attacks to Caesar's rear as well as to organize his soldiers to harry the Roman forces as they moved inland.

The events which led up to the Claudian invasion are known only in limited detail from a variety of sources but they indicate that Catuvellaunian power was growing at the expense of other Belgic tribes, principally the Trinovantes in Essex and the Atrebates in Berkshire, Hampshire and Sussex. This situation was brought to an end by the Claudian invasion in AD 43 but it would be wrong to assume that Catuvellaunian expansion would otherwise have continued unchecked. It is more likely that Catuvellaunian power was just a phase in a ceaseless, episodic sequence of fluctuations in tribal power, more dependent on the prestige and status of individual kings than any absolute regional advantage.

So we have a vivid impression of tribal groups engaged in long-term territorial disputes fought out between the ruling families and their associates. This may reflect a real pressure on land and competition for control of the richest and most productive areas, a pressure which increased as the potential to spend the surplus on imported goods grew. On the other hand these disputes may simply reflect the posturing ambitions of a military élite who continually fabricated disputes as excuses for trials of strength.

The archaeological evidence

We can only understand the prehistoric period through the remains of its settlements and material goods which survive in the ground. It is almost impossible to associate any one site with the limited historical information which we possess. The patterns of settlement define the areas which were occupied and our only means of distinguishing localized groups is by identifying regional variations in the form, decoration and type of manufactured articles which turn up on excavated sites. Typical examples are pottery and bronze brooches. However, such classifications are based on subjective assessments made by archaeologists and often create as many problems as they resolve. In the absence of hard historical fact it is all too easy to assume that the distribution of particular artefacts is an accurate reflection of the distribution of peoples. A modern example is the wide dispersal in the West of electronic goods manufactured in the Far East. We all know that this is a consequence of trade, and not because of mass migrations. But earlier this century prehistoric archaeology was founded on theories of movements of people across Europe, many of which were derived from examinations of the artefact record.

Inter-tribal tension, real or imagined, was expressed in the landscape by fortified centres which were used to control the landscape. The most prominent features of the Iron Age landscape were the hillforts. They vary in size and distribution, for example they are more or less absent from the east and north, but all share the common characteristic of being defended hill-top sites. Some are small and simple with a single bank and ditch, and are called 'univallate', while others, like Maiden Castle and Danebury in their final forms, were substantial enclosures with complex entrances and several

2 *Reconstructed view of the hillfort at Maiden Castle (Dorset) as it may have appeared during the early part of the first century* AD. *(Paul Birkbeck; English Heritage.)*

banks and ditches, called 'multivallate' (**2**). Few interiors have been closely examined but those which have, like Danebury and Hod Hill, show that they contained many probable dwellings and other evidence of long-term occupation, such as grain storage pits (**3**).

As a phenomenon the hillforts date back to the early part of the first millennium BC; towards the end of that millennium some of the hillforts, and Maiden Castle is the classic example, were enlarged and had their defences elaborated. This seems to have coincided with a reduction in the number of hillforts in occupation, so it seems that either some regional groups were being successful at the expense of others, or that efforts were being concentrated at a smaller number of sites in the interests of efficiency.

Hillforts tell us nothing about why they were

3 *Reconstructed view of huts within Maiden Castle (see also* **2***).* (Miranda Schofield; English Heritage.)

13

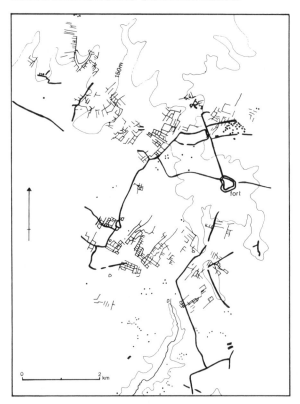

4 *Plan of the Iron Age hillfort at Sidbury (Hampshire) and its surrounding territory marked out with ditches and associated field systems. The symbol · marks a round barrow.* (After Fowler.)

built or who built them. Naturally there are no inscriptions and unfortunately ancient sources barely mention them. But their defensive nature does indicate that they were probably built to control the landscape and that society was sufficiently centralized to enable the necessary labour to be organized or coerced. We know that this was a tribal society so it seems reasonable to assume that the principal hillforts were the strongholds, perhaps episodically, of tribal leaders. The hillfort would not only supply a tribal chief with the practical benefit of a fortified base but also give him the opportunity to display his power and prestige. The men who controlled Maiden Castle for example must have been men of substance, or at least they thought they were. However, finds within hillforts of either houses or artefacts are generally unexceptional, the latter including pottery, bone and iron implements. By contrast, the many wealthy burials of the period, for example at

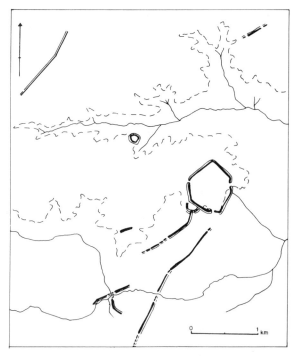

5 *Plan of the Iron Age* oppidum *at Silchester. Note the central main area which subsequently approximated in part to the Roman town, and the additional ditches which demarcated large areas of the surrounding land.* (After Boon.)

Welwyn Garden City, are associated with rural areas or sites rather than hillforts. This makes it more difficult to see hillforts as the strongholds of the wealthy, though of course very few have been excavated in detail. Perhaps hillforts served instead as seasonal refuges for the surrounding rural population.

At Sidbury near Chisenbury Warren (Hampshire) the hillfort has been shown to lie at the centre of a system of fields and ditches which radiate from it (**4**). The ditches split the land into blocks which were sub-divided into fields, and open areas perhaps used for pasture. The system remained in use in the Roman period and is an important example of rural continuity. Here we can see archaeological evidence for a hillfort being the focal point of a regional landscape.

About the beginning of the first century AD the Belgic tribes of south-eastern Britain in particular came to favour low-lying fortified settlements, known as the *oppida*. Some can still be observed today, for example at *Calleva* (Silchester) (**5**) and *Camulodunum* (Colchester)

where rivers and dykes define large areas of territory. These also served as tribal centres and while many were used as the basis for Roman regional capitals they bore little resemblance to towns, though many contain evidence for occupation, including industry, especially at Sheepen within the *Camulodunum* system. Instead they were probably seasonal bivouacs, markets or occasional refuges in times of danger. The presence of expensive imported goods such as fine Italian pottery or wine *amphorae*, usually found in graves, shows that they were used and controlled by people of high status. Caesar encountered similar settlements which he described as being defended refuges within a maze of forests and marshes, to which the defenders withdrew with their cattle. But, like the hillforts, they show a degree of centralization in prehistoric society, an interpretation reinforced by the evidence of chieftain coinage which bears the name of kings and the *oppida*.

The use of coinage is not only important because it is indicative of an emerging maturity in terms of standardized values and exchange (though in fact it probably had a primary value as a means of storing wealth). Some of the coinage issued by a number of tribes bears the name of the incumbent ruler, occasionally a reference to his lineage, the name of the tribe and possibly the location of the mint. Some of these can be directly linked to the personalities referred to in the historical sources which described incidents running up to and during the Claudian invasion of AD 43. A good example is a coin issued by Verica of the Atrebates bearing the legends VERICA REX, and COMMI.F which mean 'Verica, King, son of Commius'. Commius ruled the Atrebates between about 35 and 20 BC, Verica about AD 10 to 40. The coins further support the idea that the tribes were hierarchical and had hereditary ruling families. Their distribution has sometimes been argued to represent spheres of territorial influence. Although this is possible in concentrations where coins of a single tribe proliferate, isolated finds have little value in this respect.

Even if they were dominant in terms of scale and appearance the 'nucleated' sites like hillforts and *oppida* could hardly have been used by more than a small proportion of the population. Caesar described a landscape dotted with buildings and while many possible sites have been identified, few have been excavated. The classic Iron Age settlement site is still Little Woodbury in Wiltshire (6), though more recent excavations, for example at Gussage All Saints, have added to the picture. These sites were the basis of the Iron Age countryside and from them the landscape was farmed. The principal characteristics of sites like these were some sort of enclosure, either a palisade or ditch, around an area which contained buildings such as a timber and thatched round-house, storage pits and other structures now represented only as post-holes. Artefactual remains generally include pottery, quernstones, and loomweights – all evidence of the processing of agricultural produce – and sometimes evidence of cottage industry manufacturing. Gussage All Saints for example contained important evidence for the manufacture of bronze chariot fittings. Quernstone manufacturing sites which had Iron Age origins have been located at Lodsworth in West Sussex and Folkestone in Kent (see p.92).

Interpreting small settlement sites is fraught with problems because it is difficult to determine which structures were occupied at the same time, and even which features actually represent structures at all. However, the sites could be long-lived. Gussage All Saints was occupied from the fourth century BC to at least the first century AD. At Barton Court Farm in Oxfordshire Late Iron Age occupation was succeeded by a Roman farmstead which remained in use throughout the Roman period (7). In recent years it has become clear that rural farmsteads formed the vast bulk of settlements even in Roman Britain and were where most of the population would have passed their lives. The only archaeological difference is that during the Roman period Iron Age structures were often replaced by rectangular houses and sites had more frequent access to manufactured goods as a result of Roman trade. But even at the best of times this was in relatively small amounts. From an archaeological point of view this means that all these simple country sites are extremely difficult to date, and difficult to differentiate culturally because there is so little specific or idiosyncratic material, like Gaulish samian ware (see 82), to work from.

The implication of this widespread settlement, and the exports which Strabo mentions, is that prehistoric Britain was enjoying the fruits of productive agriculture. This is reflected in the archaeological record, particularly in

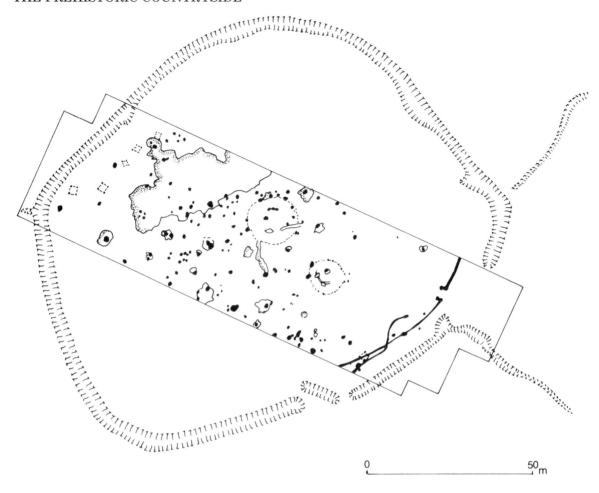

0 _____ 50 m

6 *Plan of the Iron Age homestead enclosure site at Little Woodbury (Wiltshire). Occupation began around 400–300 BC and survives in the form of hut plans, storage pits and a surrounding ditch which succeeded earlier palisades. A 'classic' excavation, Little Woodbury has been regarded as a type site for the period.* (After Bersu.)

the form of pollen evidence, which suggests that from somewhere around 500 BC there may have been widespread clearance of forests, making way for crops like hulled barley and spelt wheat. Remains of field systems also provide evidence for agriculture. The division of land into fields can sometimes be identified, for instance over large areas of north-eastern and southern England, but in most places these have been destroyed by later farming.

The traditional belief, based largely on Caesar's observation, that late prehistoric Britain was divided into an arable lowland zone and a pastoral highland zone is therefore far too simplistic. Recent studies have indicated that these field systems were being used during the late first century BC to a greater extent than ever before. Even in marginal areas like the Fens of eastern England, prehistoric settlements were much more numerous than previously thought, even though these settlements seem to have been predominantly based on pastoral farming. Either way, it seems land which might have been assumed to be marginal in a subsistence economy was being made productive in late Iron Age Britain.

Bone evidence from sites shows that pastoral farming included all the sorts of animals we would expect to find on farms today, for example sheep, cattle and pigs. On different sites

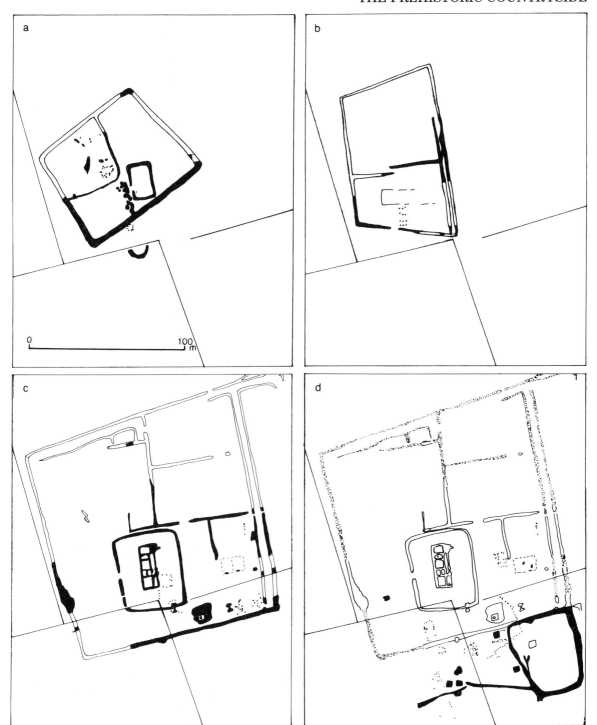

7 *Sequential plan of development at Barton Court Farm, near Abingdon (Oxfordshire). Note that while the focal point of occupation remained reasonably static until* d, *there was considerable variation in surrounding* enclosures. a *first century BC to first century AD;* b *first to second century AD;* c *late third to fourth century (villa phase – see also* **55***);* d *fifth to sixth century AD.* (After Miles.)

analysis of the bones demonstrates that sheep were reared for meat as lambs, or allowed to grow to maturity for wool. Similarly the presence of adult cattle bones implies that they were used for milk, while young bones suggest meat. So an organized tradition of animal husbandry was in existence.

Most sites display evidence for a degree of mixed farming. Naturally, the crops themselves are unlikely to survive, but tools used for processing them are commonly found, for example stone querns or iron sickles. Some of the so-called 'banjo' enclosures found within the field systems may have been used to contain stock and prevent them from wandering across fields, while breaks within the field systems may be evidence for pasture. Likewise the simple evidence of grain storage pits and loom-weights on a settlement site implies the presence of mixed farming. For a farmer in a low technology society operating pastoral and arable farming together is simple common sense. His animals provide manure for his crops, and his crops provide winter fodder for his animals. Both provide different types of security depending on the conditions but cattle had the added advantage of acting as a prestigious form of storing wealth.

Livings were even being made on marginal land, subject to the privations caused by natural catastrophes. In the Fens silt deposits suggest that occupation was intermittently disrupted by flooding, and that this became progressively worse towards the end of the Iron Age. Problems associated with water levels may have limited any attempts to operate arable farming. At Cat's Water, a settlement occupied throughout the latter part of the Iron Age, there is plenty of evidence for pastoral farming and hunting in the form of cattle, sheep, waterfowl and fish, but very little trace of cereals. The relative unpredictability of the environment may have caused periodic disruption, perhaps provoking a semi-nomadic existence for some groups.

By this period iron had succeeded bronze as the more valuable metal, principally due to its durability, but bronze was still in use for small personal ornaments or for chariot accessories. At Gussage All Saints, where a small bronze industry was in operation, the 'lost-wax' process was in use. In this method the desired object was modelled in wax with special tools and a clay mould formed around it. The mould was then heated and the wax ran out. Molten bronze was poured in and when cool the mould was broken away to reveal the raw casting. Naturally this process provides for only one finished piece per mould. There is very little evidence for iron-working on rural sites apart from the presence of slag and cinders. It undoubtedly went on, but even at Gussage these metalworking industries were almost certainly seasonal or at least peripheral to the agricultural base of a settlement.

Decorated metalwork of a military or prestigious nature is the most conspicuous and distinctive part of the late Iron Age artefact record, though compared to pottery it is rare. Finds include some fittings and accessories for chariots or horses, and swords, daggers and shields. The limited quantities of this material and its deposition in specific locations, such as wealthy graves or in concentrations in ritual water deposits shows that it was valuable and restricted to a small part of the community. It is a logical inference that such pieces belonged to a ruling class who asserted their status and social domination in the form of warrior display. The deposits in water, for example the Thames (the Battersea shield is the prime example), and other religious sites like Hayling Island, are probably to be associated either with the commemoration of deceased warriors or gifts to gods with the intention of seeking military success on an individual or group basis. The members of this upper class would have absorbed much of the limited production capacity of skilled craftsmen, such as the people working at Gussage; indeed the Gussage concern was quite possibly tied by patronage to a single group.

Pottery is the most common class of artefact found on late Iron Age sites, and by the middle of the first millennium BC major changes were taking place. At this stage pottery was still hand-made, probably for the most part at individual sites. But the appearance of a wider range of vessel forms, more elaborate decoration and better quality fabrics point to the gradual emergence of 'professional' potters, especially when some vessels can be shown to have been deposited up to a hundred miles or more from the source of the clay used. Gradually more distinctive regional styles appeared, culminating in the introduction of the wheel during the first century BC, probably via the Belgic peoples of the south-east. By the

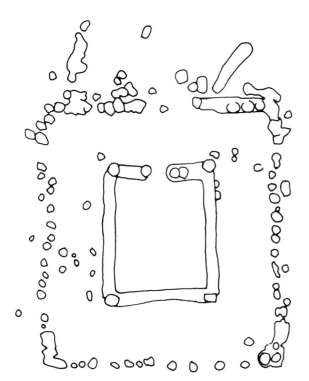

8 *Plan of the timber Iron Age temple at Heathrow (Middlesex). The plan consists of two concentric squares with an entrance facing east and closely resembles that of the later Romano-Celtic temple form.* (After Grimes.)

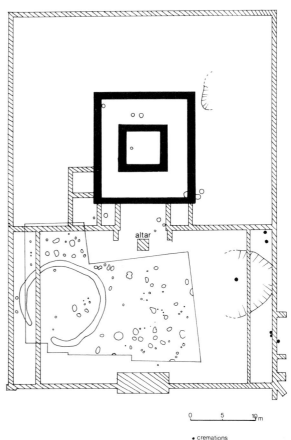

altar

0   5   10 m

• cremations

9 *Plan of the Romano-Celtic temple at Harlow (Essex) showing the relationship of the Roman structures to the Iron Age round building within the courtyard. The large numbers of Iron Age coins found in the vicinity make it likely that it was the focal point of a pre-Roman cult.* (After France, Gobel and Bartlett.)

latter part of the first century BC imported pottery had become much more widespread.

With the vast majority of the population involved in working on the land it is hardly surprising that the prehistoric countryside was a place which had a profound effect on the beliefs and customs of its inhabitants. Pre-Roman religion in Britain was concerned above all else with fertility, reproduction, physical strength and the life cycle. The powerful forces which shaped the countryside and endowed it with its productive capacities were turned into the gods of prehistory. These Celtic deities were at the heart of Romano-British religion. Very few were worshipped in buildings resembling temples, though isolated examples are known, like the shrine at Heathrow, which resembles later Romano-British temples (**8**). For the most part deities were venerated in natural locations, such as a particular tree or a spring. Often temples were sited at these places in the Roman period and they mark the synthesis of the Celtic deity with a classical equivalent. The principal example is the Celtic deity Sul, who was merged with Minerva at the sacred spring at Bath. At Harlow (Essex) recent excavations at the site of a long-known Roman temple have revealed a prehistoric building and artefacts which probably represent the focal point of a pre-Roman cult (**9**). Celtic religion held in particular regard animals thought to have special powers, for example bulls and boars, which are sometimes found in the form of bronze figurines. Such animals offered obvious symbolism both in their physical strength and perceived potency. Many of the rituals associated with these religious sites were what we would describe as superstitious, for example the practice of casting offerings into water.

11 *Bronze figurine of a Celtic fertility horse-goddess called Epona from Wiltshire. Here she is depicted with two small horses or foals and carries ears of corn and a yoke.* (British Museum.)

10 *The remaining part of the carved relief of 'Rob of Risingham', probably a hunter god of pre-Roman origin called Cocidius cut into the living rock during the Roman period close to the out-post fort at Risingham.*

By contrast, representations of the human form are rare and only during the Roman period do some of these deities appear more regularly in the archaeological record, like the warrior god Cocidius (**10**) or the goddess of fertility Epona (**11**). Epona was represented as a woman but in the company of foals and with corn. Unknown in pre-Roman Britain, she was probably Gaulish in origin but there would certainly have been very similar fertility goddesses who were worshipped in the British Iron Age. Much more common though were the so-called 'mother goddesses'. Generally unnamed and frequently depicted in threes, these took the form of female figures nursing babies or holding the products of working the land such as fruit and bread. Again the symbolism is obvious. These deities had their origins in the prehistoric countryside where the power of fertility was the single most important force in everyone's life. Fertility was admired, revered and feared because it was the key to survival.

The Roman perception of the British countryside

As mentioned above, the Greek geographer Strabo tells us that Britain exported some of its natural resources and agricultural produce. The archaeological evidence, mainly from graves, shows that the reciprocal part of this trade included a great deal of fine ware pottery, for example Arretine ware made at and around Arezzo in Italy in the late first century BC and early first century AD. Other goods included *amphorae*, shipped in for their contents like wine and fish sauce, as well as fine metal tablewares.

Trade took the form of the export of basics in return for imports of manufactured and luxury goods from the classical world; this reflects our perception of a tribal chieftain society in late Iron Age Britain. The ruling élite controlled the production of basic foodstuffs and natural resources and tapped off the surplus for their own benefit, selling it to continental traders in return for goods unobtainable in Britain. Of course we have no idea of how the goods were taken from the farmers but compulsion is certain and coercion probable. It is likely that a proportion of produce was seized whether it was 'surplus' to the farmers' requirements or not. However, the generally widespread evidence for expanding and improving agriculture makes it likely that the agricultural surplus was becoming a fact of life, even if the structure of tribal society meant that the benefits were enjoyed by a limited proportion of the population. The distribution of *amphorae*, for example, is very localized, with concentrations across the southern part of East Anglia and along the south coast between Portland Bill and where Portsmouth now lies.

On the face of it this trade cycle seems to be a perfectly satisfactory arrangement from Rome's point of view. Strabo even goes on to say that the costs of garrisoning Britain would be counter-productive because the revenue thus gained would be less than the duties already imposed on exported goods from Britain following Caesar's expeditions. So we need to consider whether the Roman government in 43 believed that conquering the island would be beneficial, and whether the benefits included exploiting the countryside.

Claudius (41–54) thought that conquering Britain would increase his personal prestige. Caligula (37–41) had planned the expedition but failed to see it through because of both his own unpredictable personality and a mutiny by his troops. Claudius, popularly regarded as an affable buffoon, needed a boost to his image. In Britain itself the territorial ambitions of the rulers of the Catuvellauni, were threatening other tribes. These included the Atrebates, a tribe which had been allied to Rome since the time of Augustus. Verica, ruler of the Atrebates, fled to Rome and begged for help, supplying Claudius with a pretext for invasion.

This was very convenient for Claudius but it only helps us form a picture of the public face of contemporary politics. Stated intentions are all very well, but such enormous decisions usually have a much more significant and unspoken aspect. Britain was, and is, a fertile place with a temperate climate. Despite the general unpredictability of the climate on a day-to-day basis the moderating influence of the Gulf Stream means that Britain's weather almost never reaches the extremes experienced by other places at the same latitude, for example in north-east America. Correspondingly, agriculture rarely suffers to a truly disastrous extent. Much later on in the province's history this would be cited as one of the principal reasons for recapturing the island when it was seized by a would-be, and self-appointed, emperor called Carausius (286–93).

Britain also had natural resources in the form of precious and base metals. Iron ore from the Weald of Kent was being exploited during the Iron Age. As early as AD 49 lead was being extracted in the Mendips and dispersed in the form of pigs, stamped with the Claudius' imperial titles for that year. Lead had enormous value as the only readily available substance with qualities of plasticity, making it useful for pipes and sealing the walls and floors of baths. The extraction of lead also yields silver, though in a very much smaller amount. Silver coinage was, at the time, the most important component of Roman coinage and served as the basic unit of exchange. Cornish tin had been shipped out of Britain since at least the late fourth century BC. Wales and the southwest also have deposits of copper (Caesar mentions its export), zinc and gold. The prospect of controlling these sources of metals may have added to the attraction. However, the distribution of metal sources, with the exception of Wealden iron, is almost exclusively in the highland zone of Britain. Some scholars believe that Rome's initial scheme behind the invasion was to restrict occupation to the lowland zone only, and that therefore control of minerals was not a motive. There is some evidence to support this in the form of the Fosse Way which runs between Lincoln and Exeter. It appears to have served as some sort of frontier by the late 40s AD, separating the highland and lowland zones, though it was soon given up in favour of a more total conquest.

It is unlikely that the Roman government viewed Britain as a venture which would prove profitable purely in terms of crop yields and mineral resources. Appian, writing around the middle of the second century, observed that though Rome controlled the most important part of Britain it had produced very little revenue. Not until the late third century do we begin to see signs that Britain was paying its way. The countryside shows little indication of speedy development despite the rapid exploitation of some metal deposits. It is much more likely that the decision to invade was based on a variety of political considerations which included: gaining prestige for Claudius; being seen to support one's allies against a foe (the Catuvellauni) bent on increasing its power by force; and making use of the army Caligula (37– 1) had raised in the form of two new legions to invade Britain. Leaving them in Gaul would have meant that there were enough soldiers on the northern frontier (Tacitus records that there were 8 legions on the Rhine in AD 23, almost a third of the total) to form a very substantial private army for anyone bent on making a bid to become emperor. Any financial gains in the form of metals or other exports can be regarded as incidental rather than acting as a primary motive. We should note that the Claudian army, which consisted of at least 40,000 men, would have been fed with food obtained in Britain. They would` therefore at the very least have had a dis-ruptive effect on any export trade in cereals if nothing else.

So in the year 43 the British countryside was serving as the economic and social foundation of a tribal society. Agriculture in both its main forms was being practised in many parts of the island and it had undoubtedly reached an organized and disciplined level. There was a certain amount of influence from the continent of Europe and this came in the form of immigrants and tools. The actual land itself had been subjected to forest clearance and the creation of field systems and was being worked from an enormous number of individual farmsteads. The tribal élites were primarily engaged in the pursuit of territorial quarrels and for the main part this is reflected in the form of large nucleated settlements which probably served as regional centres and refuges. They also creamed off some of the produce which they used to barter with merchants from the Roman Empire. From the Empire's point of view Britain's countryside presented a certain amount of potential interest but it is unlikely that this played more than a marginal role in the decision to invade.

2

Rural change in the first and second centuries

The conquest

The progress of the Roman army across southern Britain was rapid and decisive following the invasion in the summer of 43. There was little long-term active resistance as the British tribes swiftly substituted realism for idealism. The army, somewhere around 40,000 strong, had landed in east Kent at Richborough and moved westwards to fight a battle at the river Medway and then on to the Thames in the vicinity of what is now London. There the advance was halted until the Emperor Claudius arrived with his entourage from Rome to lead the march on Colchester (*Camulodunum*).

One of the four legions, the XX, stayed at *Camulodunum* and the other three, the II, the IX and the XIV split up to advance out across the new province. We know that the II moved into the south-west. Other evidence from later legionary fortresses indicates that the IX headed north while the XIV moved into the Midlands. By the year 47 most sustained British resistance in the lowland part of Britain had been quashed and some sort of frontier was established on the line of the Fosse Way which runs approximately from Lincoln to Exeter. It may have always been a temporary arrangement, or it possibly was planned to be permanent. It turned out to be temporary. This was partly because Caratacus, a son of Cunobelinus of the Catuvellauni, had moved into Wales from where he led a brief struggle at the head of the Welsh tribes. The new Roman governor, Ostorius Scapula, moved up the XX legion to the front and defeated Caratacus.

Unfortunately for Rome the areas beyond the Fosse Way turned out to be less easy to subdue. The Welsh tribes continued to cause trouble for a further thirty years. In the north the Brigantes (who occupied most of northern England) had been recognized as a client tribe. By this arrangement they were allowed to be autonomous so long as they were loyal to Rome. The Brigantian queen, Cartimandua, respected the arrangement; her husband, Venutius, did not. This led to tribal risings and subsequently intervention by Rome. The catastrophe in 60 of the Boudican Revolt by the East Anglian Iceni, another client tribe, could have led to the loss of the province. It did not because the rebellion was so ruthlessly put down that any residual resistance was terminated and it was followed by a reformed political initiative to make romanization more palatable.

Campaigns thereafter were concentrated in Wales and the north, and apart from temporarily garrisoning the areas involved in the Boudican Revolt (principally East Anglia) the central, southern and eastern part of Britain became effectively peaceful for the rest of the Roman period. For the north and west peace was more elusive, a fact frequently referred to indirectly on the coinage of the second century (**12**). Some of the effects of the permanent military presence on the countryside of the north and west will be considered in a later chapter but we need to look first at what the effect had been in rural parts of the settled zone.

The consequences of invasion

Before the Roman army arrived, the population of the countryside was made up of individuals and families who lived in a primarily subsistence economy. Although there would have been obligations to hand over some of their produce to tribal leaders (who then traded it on the continent in return for manufactured goods), many of these farming establishments

23

12 *Coin of Hadrian (117–38) struck about the year 120 with a reverse depicting the defeated province of* Britannia. *Diameter 25mm (1in).*

13 *Milestone found 11km (7 miles) west of a fort at Caerhun,* Kanovium (Gwynedd). *The inscription records that the stone was erected during the reign of Hadrian (117–38) about the year 120–21. The last two lines record that the place is 8 miles* (M[ilia] P[assuum] VIII) *from Caerhun (A KANOVIO). Milestones like this would have been placed all the way along roads in Roman Britain though few now survive. Height 1.66m (5½ft).* (British Museum.)

would have had little need to move either themselves or their products about. In other words marketing and trade were both limited and very localized as far as the bulk of the population was concerned. This was reflected in the lack of both towns and a sophisticated network of communications, as well as the general absence of imported goods on ordinary farmsteads. Within ten years of the Roman conquest the whole structure of the landscape had entirely changed, even if the nature of individual settlements was much as it had been. Where there had been traditional track-ways and occasional contact with goods or individuals from the classical world, there were now nascent towns and markets, roads (**13**), and thousands of Roman soldiers and officials.

The background to the Boudican Revolt tells us a little of the exploitative effect of this influx. Colchester had been established as a *colonia*, a device whereby retired soldiers were granted a city and land in conquered territory which they could run on a Roman model. This suited their tastes and was convenient for the government which not only had a working advertisement of cultured Roman living according to the rule of law, but also had a trained reserve of troops.

Tacitus' account tells us that the colonists had acted in a less than sympathetic way towards the native Trinovantes who lived in the vicinity of Colchester. Many of these people had had their lands seized by the colonists, which presumably means they had been expelled from their farmsteads and deprived of the means to support themselves. Recent analysis of the road system to the west of Colchester has shown how it may have formed part of centuriated land divisions right across the Gosbecks site to the south-west of the colony. Gosbecks was the focal part of the sprawling *oppidum* and almost certainly contained shrines (there were a number of temples here during the Roman period). If this area had been divided up for the colonists' benefit then it would have clearly featured high in the natives' list of grievances.

No doubt this kind of abuse of power was matched elsewhere, though probably to a lesser and more isolated extent. This is important because Roman provincial government was dependent on convincing native populations that being part of the Roman world was to their advantage. In this way existing hierarchies and social institutions could be adapted to a Roman model. People with local power retained it, or at least believed that they did, and consequently saw their path to status and wealth in terms of the hierarchy of Roman provincial administration. The same principle was operated during the nineteenth and early twentieth centuries in some of the European colonies in Africa and the East. For ordinary people the insecurity of the prehistoric landscape was replaced with the stability of the Roman world which protected them from the excesses of tribal chiefs and the privations of tribal wars. So, if the new rulers were also ruthless then provincial government would be impossible and this was what led to the Boudican Revolt.

Even with the Revolt put down there were still abuses. In particular when Agricola became governor in 78 he found that farmers were being obliged to hand over excessive amounts of food to the army (see p.86). Agricola stopped this practice but it is likely that instances of exploitation continued wherever military individuals saw an opportunity to increase their income. However, Tacitus, who recounted this episode in his *Life of Agricola*, was keen to show his father-in-law in the best possible light so it may

be that the situation was not as bad as he described it.

Political and social consolidation

A deliberate policy of positive reconstruction followed the suppression of the Boudican Revolt. Agricola's remedial measures against grain requisition abuse were part of this long-term approach. The new province, in the lowland zone at least, now seems to have entered a protracted phase of romanization designed to integrate the whole population. Primarily this took the form of urban development and one of the most striking features of the latter part of the first century and early part of the second is the reconstruction of towns destroyed in 60 (Colchester, London and Verulamium), and the public building projects in those towns.

It is difficult to be certain about who formed the populations of these new towns but the most important aspect is that they were the hubs of a provincial infrastructure of communications and administration. The countryside was unavoidably affected. Both it and the towns became inextricably linked in an economic cycle of dependence and mutual stimulation. The towns acted as concentrations of demand as markets, and as sources of manufactured goods which were either imported or made there. The countryside benefited from this and over the succeeding centuries a portion of the rural population came to do extremely well out of the arrangement, though rural development was much slower than in the towns. Few places in the lowland part of Britain lay at distances of more than 65km (40 miles) from urban centres and many were much closer. Many rural settlements show signs of experiencing more widespread access to inter-provincial trade. The minor farmstead located at Leafy Grove in west Kent is a case in point. Although the standard of living here was modest, the cremation cemetery showed that small quantities of Gaulish samian were purchased for use there, something which would have been unusual fifty years before. Only in exceptional areas like the Fens and Salisbury Plain did development remain at a native level for significantly longer, though this was probably for special reasons.

The tribal élite were an important part of developing the province. For the most part their path to maintaining their status lay in the *civitas* capitals. These were towns which were

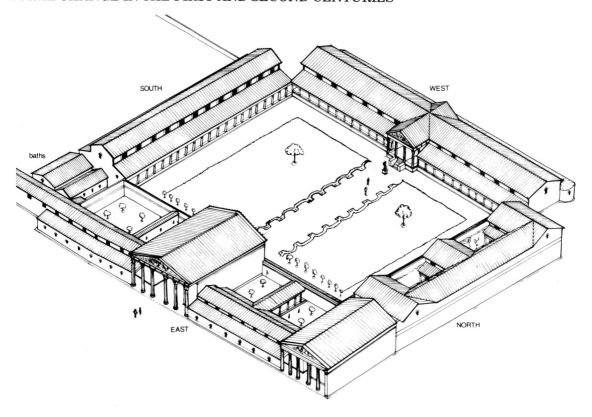

14 *Reconstructed isometric view of the so-called palace at Fishbourne, near Chichester (West Sussex) as it may have appeared in the latter part of the first century* AD. *Although not quite symmetrical the main axis of the building was marked by the entrance hall in the east wing at centre left and an 'audience chamber' in the centre of the west wing on the opposite side. Note the ornamental garden and the enclosed open courtyards, typical of contemporary Mediterranean houses.*

instituted as tribal capitals for areas which approximated to the pre-Roman tribal zones. It is no coincidence that many of these lay on or close to the site of the principal *oppidum*, as at Silchester, or hillfort, as at Dorchester, of the tribal area. There were also the client kingdoms, some of which have already been mentioned; there were at least three in Roman Britain but none outlived the first century. A client kingdom was a device to secure an area without occupying it. The tribal chief guaran-

teed his loyalty because he recognized that it was in his interests to do so. The most prominent in Roman Britain was Cogidubnus, king of the Atrebates, who is mentioned both on an inscription from Chichester and in Tacitus' writings.

Housing in the countryside: villas

The appearance of a small number of large and well-appointed houses of Roman type in the countryside in the mid to late first century has been linked to members of tribal élites and ruling houses. Houses such as these are absent from the towns at this date. Fishbourne (**14**) is the most important and from its discovery it has been linked with Cogidubnus. The site was initially associated with the army – a supply depot of sorts seems to have been established here during the Claudian period. The II legion is known to have been active in the south and south-west at this time so it was probably connected with this part of the campaign. During the 60s a large house was built here which featured mosaic floors, marble veneers and

15 *Hypocaust at Fishbourne, inserted into the north wing towards the end of the third century, just before the building's destruction by fire.*

stucco on the walls, a bath-suite and a colonnaded garden. All this was extraordinary for Britain at the time, either for towns or the countryside. There is absolutely no doubt that it belonged either to a favoured native or a Roman of high rank and wealth.

Curiously the house was occupied for barely more than ten years. By the year 75 it had been incorporated into an even more imposing house built on four wings surrounding an ornamental garden. This is the house whose remains can be viewed today. It is known to have had outbuildings as well as terraced gardens which ran down to the sea nearby. This is the house which is sometimes described as the palace of Cogidubnus. However, there is not a shred of evidence for this apart from the circumstantial evidence of its location within his territory. It is equally possible that the house was an official residence of the governor of the province,

though the same lack of evidence applies.

Fishbourne must have been built at enormous cost because many of the building materials were imported and it is probable that much of the skilled workforce was also brought in to build both houses. Not only that but to build the larger house the whole site had to be levelled and carefully prepared. Fishbourne underwent many structural alterations until its destruction by fire at the end of the third century (**15**). Unfortunately not enough is known about the general locality to associate the house with an estate around the time that it was built. It may have been surrounded by subsidiary agricultural establishments, but it is unlikely that these contributed significantly to the house's existence. Fishbourne was built as a 'no expense spared' establishment and it is a great pity that no firm evidence survives to explain its existence.

At Eccles, near Maidstone (Kent), a corridor house with a dozen rooms was put up around the year 65. There were also traces of Iron Age occupation on the site. The house was much smaller than Fishbourne but seems to have had

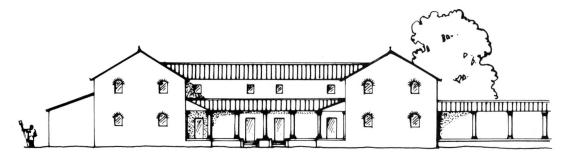

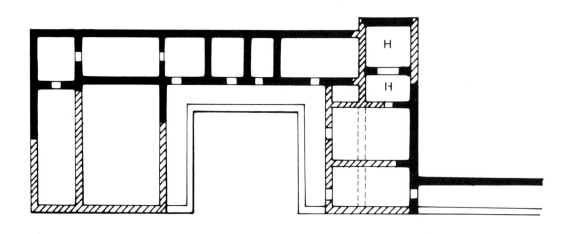

16 *Reconstructed facade of one of the early second-century houses at Rivenhall (Essex). (After Rodwell.)*

several mosaic floors, an ornamental garden of sorts and a detached bath-suite. These alone mean that it was in a different class from other rural stone houses being erected during the latter part of the first century. The house had a long history, with various alterations and additions taking place into the fourth century. As at Fishbourne a link has been suggested with a prominent member of a native tribe, though in this case there is no known candidate. The principal difference is that Eccles appears to have had a commercial base to its existence. Pottery was being manufactured nearby and production included vessels which are typical of

the period, and copied types that were being manufactured on the continent, for example flagons, *mortaria* and platters. The market may have been civil, military or both and the house may therefore have belonged to someone who had spotted an opportunity. This is likely to have been a person of Gaulish or Italian origin who moved into Britain once the Boudican Revolt was suppressed, though the pre-Roman occupation evidence makes a British candidate plausible.

Rivenhall lies in the heart of Trinovantian territory in Essex. It is one of a number of sites in the area which have yielded fine decorated Belgic bronze mirrors from the pre-Conquest period. This and other settlement evidence, such as field systems, points to it having been the home of a reasonably affluent Trinovantian family. During the Roman period an extensive villa complex was built, dating back at least to the beginning of the second century (**16**). No structural traces of the late Iron Age buildings were located but pottery, enclosure ditches and pits are evidence of the presence of a Belgic farmstead, similar to many others known in the area. There was no structural evidence for a late first-century Roman-type house, but the early second-century buildings, unusual in any case, were associated with evidence for the demolition of an earlier Roman-type house. This included broken roof tiles used as hard-core, and shattered wall-plaster beneath mortar layers of the second-century house. It may be that this was an instance of a Trinovantian family benefiting from the Roman invasion, and subsequently from the post-Boudican reconstruction. As the conquest was purported to be a measure to counter Catuvellaunian expansion (which had been at Trinovantian expense), and the Trinovantes had suffered privations caused by the Colchester colonists, this is an interesting idea. It is, unfortunately, nothing more than just that.

Housing in the countryside: farmsteads

The villas at Fishbourne, Eccles and Rivenhall cannot easily be linked to the developing agricultural economy of the Romano-British countryside; they are far too immediate. Instead it seems more likely that they owe their existence to existing capital or commercial opportunities, in other words the homes of philo-Roman tribal aristocrats, Roman officials or even merchants. A much more common feature of the countryside was the gradual romanization of an existing native farmstead. Roman villa sites often show that they had pre-Roman structures underneath. The small villa at Brixworth (Northamptonshire) is one such case. Here a very simple stone house with four rooms (though it may have had an upper storey too) was put up during the last thirty years of the first century (**17**). It lay immediately beside a round house of earlier date. It should be remembered though that the round house continued in use at many sites for a very long time, sometimes never falling out of use, for example at Winterton in Lincolnshire. Tradition and its utilitarian nature meant that this form was far from being made obsolete as soon as rectangular houses became more common.

The Brixworth house never developed into

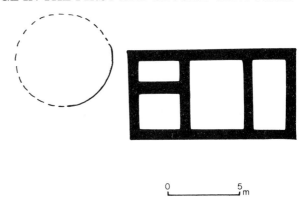

0 _____ 5 m

17 *Plan of the house at Brixworth (Northamptonshire), in its late first-century phase and showing the location of an earlier round house which the stone building replaced. (See also* **56***; After Turland.)*

anything elaborate but by the end of the second century it had been extended with an additional room, with further embellishments added during the fourth century (see **56**). At Quinton, also in Northamptonshire, a rectangular house was built directly over an early first-century round house. Here there must have been a break in occupation, however brief. There are many other houses which show the same change from a native structure to a romanized rectangular structure, such as Park Street and Lockleys (Hertfordshire) during the first century, or even as far west as Whitton in south Wales by the second century. In cases where earlier structural remains have not been located, for example at Lullingstone and Plaxtol (Kent), site finds point to there having been an earlier house. At Lullingstone a reasonably elaborate winged-corridor stone house was built by the year 90 on a small terrace above the river Darenth. It was probably linked to a farm because one of its rooms had a cellar accessed by a ramp from outside (**18**). Its use as a grain store seems quite likely and as such it falls into the tradition of storing grain in subterranean chambers, originating in the grain storage pits associated with Iron Age farmsteads. However, by the second century this room may have been converted into a domestic shrine when a niche was cut into the wall and painted with a group of water nymphs (**colour plate 11**).

Replacing a native round house with a rectangular version with at least stone fittings is not necessarily the only form of evidence for

18 *The north end of the villa at Lullingstone (Kent), showing the stair case which descended to the 'Deep Room' where the marble busts (**60**) were deposited. Note the later blocking.*

change on a rural site. A number of apparently free-standing stone bath-houses are known, often described as 'isolated'. There was no alternative to stone for bath-houses because of the risk of fire and the effects of warm damp air on timber structures. It is quite probable that they in fact belonged to houses which were built of timber and have therefore not survived in easily recognizable form. The simple timber-framed house requires nothing more substantial than a series of shallow slots cut into the ground for cill beams. It was a perfectly satisfactory and extremely common way of building houses throughout the Roman period and on into the Middle Ages. If the house is physically dismantled then the archaeological traces are likely to be minimal. One such 'isolated' bath-house in Orpington (Kent) lies on an east-facing slope above the river Cray. The various finds from the site indicate that it may have

been in occupation from the late first century, though it cannot be shown that the bath-house is this early. Another, not far away at Baston Manor, was more certainly built in the early second century and possibly even before. Both are likely to have formed part of small farmsteads, centred on timber houses which have so far proved elusive. Such home 'improvements' were supported by a growing industry of specialists, such as the flue-tile maker Cabriabanus who worked in Kent in the second century, and the tile kiln associated with the villa at Ashtead in north-east Surrey around the same time (see pp.83) (**19** and see **69**).

Increasing prosperity was expressed not only by building better houses, or at least augmenting the facilities. Personal and household possessions are an important index of wealth. As shown in Chapter 1, during the late Iron Age fine pottery and other tablewares from the Continent are generally only found in wealthy graves. They are rare on occupation sites of any type, but on rural sites of early Roman date, particularly those where structural remains point to at least a modest degree of improvement,

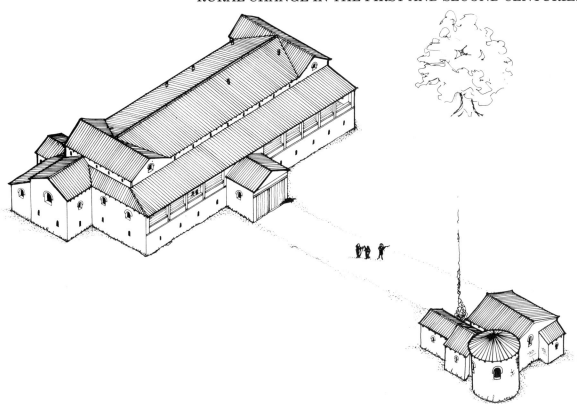

19 *Reconstructed isometric view of the house and detached bath-house at Ashtead (Surrey), the centrepiece of an estate which seems to have earned part of its income from the manufacture of decorated flue-tiles. (See also* **79**.)

pottery and other manufactured goods do appear much more frequently. But it is worth bearing in mind that the towns of the late first century produce enormous quantities of goods by comparison. The countryside was beginning to participate in the Roman marketing structure but lagged some way behind the towns. The Lullingstone house for example became exceptional for special reasons in its later years but during the late first and second centuries it was a modest and unprepossessing house, though it had the advantage of being close to London and the main road between London and the Kent coast at Richborough. This convenient location meant that the owners were able to enjoy the use of imported samian pottery and wine *amphorae* from Gaul and *amphorae* from Spain which probably contained olive oil.

The Bignor villa in West Sussex became a place of local prominence in the fourth century (see **40**). But like the Lullingstone house it has produced a limited amount of evidence for prosperity of sorts in the late first and second centuries; this also included samian, dating to the late first century, coins and brooches. Structural remains of this period have proved largely elusive but traces of a timber-framed building have been identified. So even if the house was modest at this early date the small number of finds shows that the occupants had the use of coinage and were able to buy pottery which had been manufactured in Gaul. For relatively ordinary people this kind of commercial choice would have been less readily available fifty years before. It is difficult for us to appreciate what sort of difference this made to the rural population but it is clear that the standard of living for a significant proportion had changed out of all recognition.

During the second century imported and other manufactured goods become significantly more common in small villas. A modest winged-corridor house at Sedgebrook, Plaxtol, suffered a small fire some time towards the end of the second century. The fire burnt out a room at the north end of the house and the internal fittings, including a wooden floor, collapsed into

20 *The second-century winged corridor house at Plaxtol (Kent), during excavation looking south-west. In the foreground is one of the wing rooms.*

a small cellar immediately below (**20**). The owners abandoned the cellar and left the burnt filling where it was. During excavation this was found to contain the remains of several mid-second-century samian bowls (see **82**), glass vessels, a glass window and a silver spoon of first- or second-century type. Apart from scattered pottery and a bronze drop handle from a cupboard, the rest of the house produced virtually no other evidence for household goods. Only the fire damage created a situation where a significant amount of material was preserved.

Plaxtol shows how misleading an archaeological excavation can be. Without the fire it might have been easy to conclude that this was a very modest establishment, owned by people who were too poor to afford quality goods. But here we can see that this relatively simple house (there were apparently no mosaics for instance) was owned by a family which had access to fine pottery and glasswares and could even afford silver spoons. Only the fire had guaranteed their preservation; it could be

deduced from this that under normal circumstances such objects would be so highly valued by the owners that they were very unlikely to be abandoned, and would therefore not appear in the archaeological record. Maintenance and the clearance of rubbish meant that the detritus of everyday life was disposed of away from the house and in the countryside it was easier to do this further away than it was in a town.

A plausible scenario in each case is a native family accumulating enough spare money and having the incentive to spend it on building a modest house of more Roman type, perhaps equipping it with a bath-house to enable them to live in a more 'romanized' way, and on purchasing manufactured goods. There was obviously a degree of social motivation and aspiration here, though it is hard to identify the precise stimulus, other than the general impact of living in a Roman province. The phenomenon is sufficiently widespread to suggest that a number of establishments were enjoying the economic benefit of being part of the Roman Empire. Of course we cannot prove that there was continuity of occupation by the same family; it may be that in some cases the original occupants had been ousted, or had fled. It is interesting that while native farming settlements have been identified well into northern Britain, the pattern of villa distribution is heavily biased to the central southern and eastern parts of the province, which was of course the most urbanized part too. The modest houses like Brixworth and Lullingstone all generally seem to belong in their primary 'Roman' phases to the last quarter of the first century. This not only reflects the period of major urban development but would also allow for the passing of a generation or two from the Conquest during which time capital was gradually accumulated and conservatism was eroded.

The background to this rural development is likely to have been economic and fiscal. The towns served not only as centres of exchange but also contained relatively large, agriculturally unproductive, populations. There is a great deal of evidence for an enormous level of imports during the late first and early second centuries in the towns, taking off around the years 70 to 75, and no doubt this was when the urban populations were at their highest rate of growth. London has been shown to have had a thriving waterfront but the evidence is naturally largely confined to imperishable ceramic goods. Some of these, mainly the *amphorae*, were imported for their food contents. Isolated finds in London do show that grain was being imported. This implies that there was not enough food available in Britain to supply the indigenous population, the army and other new arrivals who had probably gone to the burgeoning towns. If this was the case then the price of grain would have been elevated by market forces, though we have no evidence that it reached crisis levels. Imported grain was bound to be more costly, unless it was being shipped in for the army's benefit.

On a rural farmstead within reasonable reach of a town there was the opportunity to supply food to the local market. Bignor for example lies within easy reach of Chichester, a town which had been instituted as a *civitas* capital by the middle of the first century. The houses in north Kent mentioned above, like Lullingstone and Plaxtol, lay close to rivers which would have given them access to the Thames and therefore London. The government was subsidizing the province through massive imports and injections of cash via the wages of troops and administrators, and this alone necessarily implies a shortage of resources within the province. The providers of food would benefit, and

we see the results of that on the ground. Nevertheless, it would be quite wrong to imply a very rapid degree of development on farms during the first and second centuries. Whereas town-houses were being built on a larger and better-appointed scale by the late second century, the country houses show a much more gentle rate of development. The transition from round house to rectangular house with rooms can often appear to have taken place 'overnight' in archaeological terms (though in practice there may have been several years involved) but once changed, these houses often altered very little over the next five or six generations.

The appearance of villages
The word 'village' evokes an image of a small medieval English settlement made up of a cluster of houses, a scattering of farmhouses all centred on a church, a green and a pond. It is also a convenient term to describe clusters of modest Romano-British houses in small rural settlements. Unlike villa estates there is rarely a dominant house and all the buildings share a common level of limited development.

Romano-British villages have traditionally attracted very limited archaeological attention. Meaningful excavations have to be extensive and finds, especially those which can be accurately dated, are comparatively few. However, aerial and field surveys have demonstrated that there were far more of these villages than was previously thought. They began to develop during the first and second centuries, no doubt as a supplementary consequence of the growth and romanization of individual farmsteads. Small villages could have supplied some of the services which would otherwise have to be sought in towns, with their inhabitants probably farming the land about.

Development was even slower than in some of the villa sites discussed above. The round house form remained in use right up to the end of the second century at some places, for example at East Tilbury (Essex). However, at other sites, such as Catsgore (Somerset), timber-framed rectangular houses had been built by the same time. These succeeded three early second-century farms around the year 150, which lay close to one another but had polygonal timber-framed structures on stone footings contained within banked enclosures (**21**). The excavator believed that these earlier

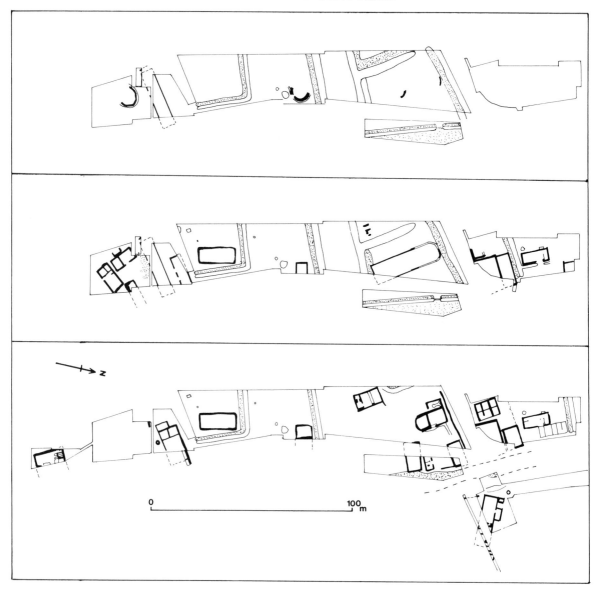

houses were likely to have been eminently serviceable and that therefore the decision to replace them with rectangular houses must have been primarily a cultural, rather than practical, one. Finds from the site show that Catsgore had access to imported goods, including second-century samian ware, and a very small quantity of *amphorae*.

At Claydon Pike (Gloucestershire) an extensive though irregular system of fields, boundaries and droveways has been identified (**22**), while around a village at Dunston's Clump (Nottinghamshire) a more regimented division of fields, described as a 'brickwork' system has

21 *Plan of the village at Catsgore (Somerset), showing the development of the excavated area through successive phases from the first/second century (upper), third century (middle), to the fourth century (lower). The site seems to have consisted of a number of distinct clusters of buildings with their own enclosures. Note the gradual emergence of rectangular buildings in distinct complexes within what remained essentially the same divisions of land. (See also **58** and **78**; After Leech.)*

22 *Plan of the village (?) settlement at Claydon Pike (Oxfordshire). The site is defined by a stream running around three sides and through a patch of marshland to the north (top). In the left centre the stippled area marks a road entering from the west and turning north before exiting the site to the north-east. The various black lines in this area mark enclosures perhaps used for corralling animals and acting as compounds for stores. Traces of buildings were found in and among these areas. (After Miles.)*

been traced from the air. The Romano-British village of Chisenbury Warren seems to have 'inherited' the field system associated with the nearby hillfort at Sidbury (see **4**). This may represent the coerced evacuation of the local population from a site they could have used as a stronghold to one which could be supervised. It was, after all, in the provincial authorities' interests to keep the annual cycle of agricultural work in full swing, rather than destroying local communities.

Imperial and official rural development

Most of the sites discussed so far are essentially 'private' in nature, even the villages. Few villages have actually been excavated sufficiently well to allow conclusions about their purpose and date to be reached. Claydon Pike is one, but the situation there now seems to have been much more complex. Here a long-established Iron Age settlement was sited on the north side of a stream. A number of round houses have been located, but during the first century BC the settlement seems to have moved across the stream to the south where it survived on into the Roman period. A major change took place around the early second century when the site was drawn into the Roman road network (see **22**). A new road some 5m (17ft) wide was built across the late Iron Age site; occupation around it seems to have been official in nature though there also seems to have been a shrine. The appearance of *amphorae* sherds shows that even a comparatively remote site like this had been brought into the Roman mechanisms of long-distance transport and trade.

Romano-British Claydon Pike included facilities for corralling animals and the storage of foodstuffs in an aisled barn contained within a compound. The site may therefore have functioned as an official centre for buying in produce for the army's consumption at fixed prices, or in lieu of taxes. The presence of a small number of military artefacts supports the idea that there may have been a detachment of soldiers stationed there, though such a link is tenuous. Evidence for another enclosure containing living quarters points to the attachment of a village-like community. The site could perhaps have been a kind of official farm with resident native labourers producing food for the government. This is speculation but the nature of the site indicates a different arrangement to that at other village or villa sites.

Working the land was not exclusively left to private Romano-British landowners. 'Imperial estates' are known throughout the Empire and were large tracts of land owned by the emperor and worked on his behalf. Roman land law also included the concept of the *ager publicus*, literally 'public land'. This land was that usually acquired by the state as a consequence of military conquest. Some was sold by auction to raise cash for the state, some was used for the establishment of colonies of military veterans (*Camulodunum* being the prime Romano-British example), and some was let to tenants on leases of varying length. Land which had been ravaged as a result of war was let on favourable terms (usually a small proportion of the produce) to those who had the capital or the will available to redevelop it but such occupants could be ejected without warning. Some estates, perhaps purchased at auction, were owned by the senatorial families of Italy who owned huge tracts of land across the Empire as we shall see later (p.73). Claydon Pike may have been one of these imperial or senatorial estates; other possible imperial estates are known and the evidence points to their development at around the same time. Clearly the ownership of land in Roman Britain could be as complicated as it is now and without the benefit of inscriptions or other documentary evidence it is not generally possible to say who actually owned anywhere.

The Fens are large areas of low-lying land in parts of Lincolnshire, Cambridgeshire and Norfolk. Prone to flooding, the Fens can only be effectively exploited for human needs if land management and organized drainage systems are operated. During the Roman period there were no towns except on the fringes, for example Water Newton, Godmanchester and Cambridge, and there also appear to have been exceedingly few villas.

The traditional view of the Fens in Roman times was that they may have formed part of an imperial estate. The lack of developed Roman settlements was taken to indicate that the native population was obliged to work under certain conditions and this restricted their ability to accumulate wealth and therefore benefit from romanization. In other words, it was an area where development was deliberately suppressed and therefore the archaeological record is impoverished compared to that from other parts of the province. However, as a result of survey and excavation work it has now become clear that the Fens were being opened up on a large scale from the early second century on.

From around the time of the Roman invasion there is a marked increase in evidence for occupation of the Fens of a late Iron Age type. Most conspicuous was the building on one of the very few areas of higher ground, Stonea Camp, an enclosure which has similarities to both hillforts and *oppida*. Coin hoards from here and the general vicinity point to occupation between about AD 40 and 60, with many of the hoards having a bias to coins of the Iceni. It has been suggested that Stonea was a major Fenland trading centre. It may also have been a major political centre for the Iceni, though we cannot attach any specific names or incidents to it. We do know that the Iceni actively resisted the Roman forces under the governor Ostorius Scapula about the year 47, even soliciting a confrontation at what Tacitus calls *agresti aggere* (a 'rustic rampart'). Subsequently it seems that the defeated Iceni were ruled by one Prasutagus who served as a client king. He died around the year 60 and it is possible that his posture towards Rome lay behind the stability which appears at Stonea Camp.

In his will Prasutagus bequeathed his lands to Rome in an effort to sustain the stability, but the ensuing oppression and land seizures which followed were fundamental reasons for the Revolt of 60, led by his widow Boudica. In the Fens this is marked by a virtual absence of material of Flavian date. Despite the successful defeat of the rebels there followed a protracted period of punitive repression of the tribes involved. While this would have involved much of East Anglia the absence of development in the Fens is especially marked.

It was not until Hadrian became emperor and visited Britain in 122 that the area was opened up once more. This is not a certain fact, but circumstantial evidence makes it likely. Across the Channel large-scale drainage works had been dug a century before, including a channel called *Drusiana*, after Drusus, to help control the outflow of the Rhine. The Fens were now also extensively drained, though this may have been aided by a natural change in conditions favouring a lowering of the water table anyway. The attraction would have been the opening up of large tracts of land which could be used for agriculture, though salt was also a major resource here too. Aerial photography points to the division of land into organized areas of fields. The Car Dyke is the most prominent drain normally associated with this phase. It ran round the western part of the Fens from Cambridge to Lincoln; smaller drains ran into it.

Much the most prominent settlement identified so far is at Stonea Grange (**23**). Unfortunately its unusual central building and associated structures have not yielded any inscriptions which might give clues to its purpose. A substantial stone tower was built here under Hadrian (**24**) and was surrounded by a number of rectangular areas divided by roads resembling the *insulae* found in towns. These contained timber buildings, fencing and other structures. The site is remarkable for its lack of evidence for production of any kind, including industry and the processing of food. However, there have been numerous imported finds of early second-century date, for example samian ware and Spanish *amphorae*, as well as quality pottery manufactured in Britain itself. A small Romano-Celtic temple has been located in the vicinity, possibly dedicated to Epona. A gold plaque dedicated to Minerva and a bronze bust of the same, found somewhere in the locality, suggest that there may have been a shrine to her too.

Stonea's purpose is obscure because it seems to have been a civilian settlement which imported everything that it needed. This points to an official role of sorts and it may be that it was an administrative centre for the Fens, perhaps controlling and overseeing maintenance of drainage and roads. In this capacity it may therefore have functioned as the headquarters (*principia*) of an imperial estate, as at Combe Down. The large numbers of coin finds may also mean that it served as a market centre. In all these respects then it could have acted as a kind of artificial town, serving both commercial and administrative interests. Curiously the entire site was cleared and levelled by about the year 200, though whether this reflected a purely political decision or one based on declining natural conditions is unknown. A number of settlement sites seem to have experienced renewed flooding at about this time though whether Stonea's abandonment was a cause or symptom, or linked at all, cannot be discerned.

The site at Grandford some 9km (6 miles) to

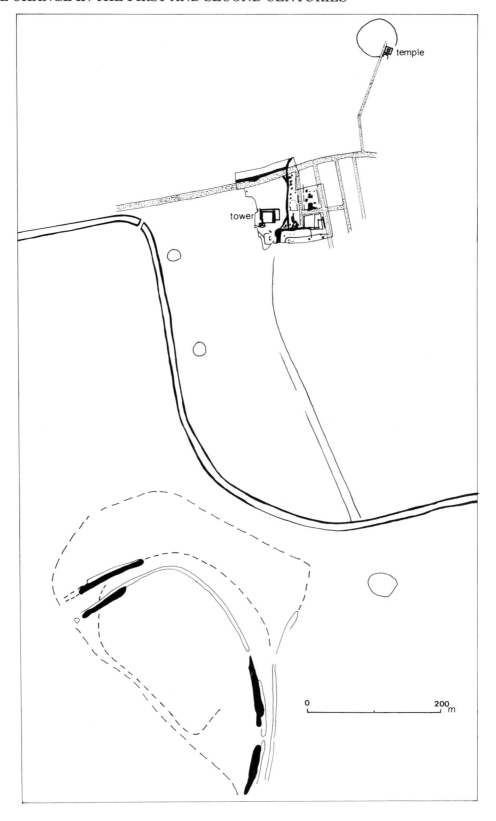

temple

tower

0   200 m

the north-west seems to represent one of the small communities which benefited from Fenland development. There were numerous similar small settlements of native or village type throughout the Fens from the second century on. At Grandford initial Roman occupation is attributed to the hypothetical presence of a fort of post-Boudican date. If so, it will have been built in order to help police the area once the Revolt had been suppressed. However, civilian occupation of the area did not appear until *c*. 90. This took the form of timber-framed buildings on earth platforms with the luxury of tile roofs. Apart from some remodelling of one structure, the site seems to have remained relatively static until somewhere between 200 and 250 when the whole area was covered with gravel and silt at least 60cm (2ft) in depth. This must represent a disastrous flood or series of floods.

Grandford was always modest, for example there are no traces of mosaics here, which means that significant prosperity was always somewhat elusive to the occupants. The excavator has equated the site with other villages of this date found throughout Roman Britain. A rural living of sorts was being made and this enabled the importation of decorated colour-coat wares. Little evidence for the economic basis of the site was found, though a number of ovens were built in the vicinity. Surface finds from Coldham, some 6km (4 miles) to the north-east included a number of iron agricultural and industrial tools, possibly of Roman date.

Salisbury Plain and Cranborne Chase

The other possible site of an imperial estate covers a large area to the south-east of Bath. Despite being bounded by roads there are no towns and only a very light scattering of villas, for example at Whatley and Hinton St Mary (**colour plate 16**), and some isolated temple sites such as Lamyatt Beacon (see **94**). Nevertheless a number of native sites have been located in the region, such as Woodcuts in north Dorset (**25**). The settlement had its origins in the years shortly before the Roman

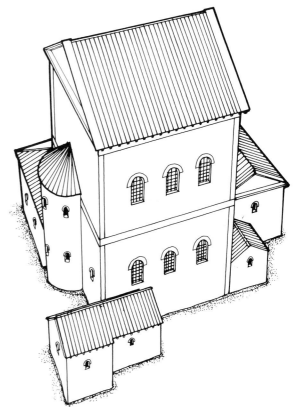

24 *The tower at Stonea as it may have appeared in the second century.*

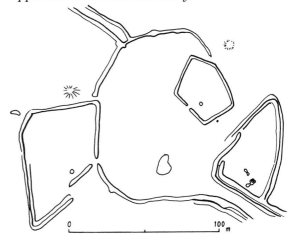

25 *Plan of the native settlement at Woodcuts (Dorset), during the second to third centuries. The distinctive features of the site are the ditches which divided up the land into various compounds. The larger will probably have been used for corralling and containing animals, while the smallest (upper right) may have been a residential area.* (After Hawkes.)

23 (Left) *Plan of the Fenland site at Stonea Grange (Cambridgeshire), showing the Iron Age settlement and the Roman buildings with temple.* (After Potter.)

conquest and remained in occupation right up until about the year 175, during which time the standard of living remained more or less unchanged. By the end of the second century, though, romanization began to have an impact, but only in the form of wall-plaster and the installation of corn-drying ovens. By way of comparison, most new town-houses at this date had stone walls, painted wall-plaster and one or two mosaic floors, as well as numerous manufactured contents such as bronze, glass and pottery utensils. Most villas at this period were also beginning to enjoy some of these benefits.

So Woodcuts, and other sites like it, were almost a century behind contemporary country houses such as Lullingstone or Park Street, and this points to a standard of living which

barely exceeded subsistence. Modern interpretation of the nineteenth-century excavation records has drawn attention to the limited number of grain storage pits, considering the size of settlement and length of duration. This suggests that a large portion of crops grown by the settlement may have been requisitioned annually and a comparison with Claydon Pike is worth considering. However, an alternative interpretation might attribute the poor rate of development to the area's relative infertility, something which is usually blamed for poor development in other more obviously remote areas such as the extreme south-west. In other words poor development cannot be regarded as automatic evidence for the existence of an imperial estate.

3

The countryside in the military zone

The historical background

From about the year 65 on, the military zone in Roman Britain was roughly equivalent to the highland zone. This remained the case until the final withdrawal of Roman troops during the early years of the fifth century. The army had a limited presence in the lowland zone after 65 but the presence of a substantial standing force always played a significant role in the economy of the Romano-British countryside everywhere.

The history of the conquest of Roman Britain tends to create a vivid impression of protracted warfare in the highland zone, especially on the northern frontier. In truth any violence was localized, seasonal and, in absolute chronological terms, brief. During the latter part of the first century the principal campaign in the north was that of Agricola who, between about 78 and 84, consolidated the efforts of his predecessors in the north of England against the Brigantes and took his forces well into northern Scotland. Not only were these lands swiftly given up after 84, including the abandonment of a new legionary fortress and many new forts, but the Romans had also done little more than make their way along the eastern coast of Scotland. For most of the tribespeople in Scotland at the time, the Roman presence must have seemed of extremely minimal significance.

Thereafter, Hadrian's Wall stabilized the frontier with a brief attempt under Antoninus Pius (138–61) to push the line further north. Septimius Severus' Scottish campaign in the early part of the third century did little more than to emulate Agricola's efforts and was similarly inconclusive. During the third century the frontier was sufficiently settled to allow many of the military installations to fall

into ruin. There were occasional transgressions of the frontier but apart from the more serious incidents towards the end of the fourth century these seem likely to have amounted to little more than light skirmishes. Northern Britain retained long-term garrisons at a number of forts, for example Binchester in County Durham, or Ribchester across the Pennines in Lancashire, and was governed from the legionary fortress and colony at York. But the presence of these strongholds is not indicative of sustained disruptive violence.

In Wales, most of the military campaigning had ceased by the beginning of Agricola's governorship in 77. Shortly before this a decision was made to build a series of permanent forts during the governorship of Sextus Julius Frontinus, for example at Brecon y Gaer and Castell Collen (Powys). These brought to an end the long period of intermittent warfare, especially against the Silures in the south. The Welsh garrisons were supervised from the legionary fortresses at Chester and Caerleon but, unlike the north, Wales seems to have been free of even occasional warfare (at least as far as the recorded history is concerned) and some of the forts like Castell Collen appear to have been empty for long periods.

The fact that a significant portion of the Roman army was permanently garrisoned in Wales and the north, whether or not any military activity was actually taking place, means that there was always a military zone. The countryside was affected in a number of ways. The army was a permanent customer for agricultural products, though the various units seem to have become gradually more self-sufficient. The network of roads was designed to connect the garrisons and to facilitate the movement of troops and transport of supplies rather than connect centres of civil population; there were fewer major roads than in the civilian part of Britain. This both reflected and discouraged the development of towns, and of course this had an effect on the development of villas. With no easily accessible commercial markets there were fewer opportunities to make money; the army either took what it needed or fixed its own price rather than the farmer's.

A glance at a map of known monuments of Roman Britain in northern England and Wales shows that towns were small and few (see 1). In south Wales, outlying towns were sited at Caerwent, Kenchester and Carmarthen, with a very small number of villas or houses, mostly hugging the southern coastline. North and central Wales seems only to have experienced romanization in the form of forts and the occasional appearance of Roman artefacts such as pottery. Northern England was similar, with towns at York, Aldborough, Brough and some civilian settlements beside the forts at, for example, Catterick, Old Carlisle, Corbridge and Chesters. Villas were slightly more numerous especially in the valleys of rivers feeding the Humber Estuary. The most northerly yet discovered lay close to the city of Durham in the valley of the river Wear.

The military zone then had a very different countryside from the civilian lowlands. Clearly a villa economy centred on the towns existed only to a very limited extent. There is no evidence for the 'imperial estates'. Despite this, as discussed in Chapter 1, there is plenty of evidence for agricultural development in the late pre-Roman Iron Age. It is difficult to avoid the conclusion that a number of factors conspired to limit rural development in the military zone during the Roman period. We should consider the words of the economist Adam Smith who observed in his *Wealth of Nations* in 1776 that, 'The mountains of Scotland, Wales and Northumberland indeed are not capable of much improvement, and seemed destined by nature to be the breeding grounds for Great Britain'. This would have been just as relevant an observation in the Roman period. Another significant feature was the presence of mineral resources, traditionally the preserve of the emperor and extracted on his behalf under military supervision. Most of Britain's major mineral resources lie in the 'highland' zone but

26 *Map of Britain showing the principal sources of the most important minerals mined during the Roman period. C copper; G gold; L lead (silver as a by-product at many locations); T tin. Note the bias to the 'highland zone' with the ironworks of the Weald in the extreme south-east being the most noticeable exception (see 29). (After various sources.)*

even those which did not, for example Wealden iron, were also administered from 'mini' military zones (**26**).

Mineral and other natural resources

Britain was exporting metals to the Continent from as early as the third century BC, and Caesar was certainly aware of the trade in mineral resources. The extent to which the promise of mineral wealth played a part in the decision to invade the island is not known, but clearly it must have supported the case for conquest. Metals were being extracted within a very few years of the invasion. A lead pig, now lost, found in the Mendips where there are deposits of silver-bearing lead, bore an inscription which includes the titles of Claudius for the year 49. Another for the same year, found in France but made of Mendip lead, also bears the titles of the II legion. Another carries the names of Vespasian and his son Titus, as well

27 *Lead pig bearing the titles of the Emperor Vespasian (69–79) and his son Titus. On the side is the abbreviated name of the Deceangli, a tribe which occupied North Wales, and which therefore tells us where the lead had been mined. Found at Hints Common (Staffordshire). Weight 71kg (about 156lb). (British Museum.)*

as the name of the tribal area from which it came, the territory of the Deceangli in north Wales (**27**). The right to extract minerals was the emperor's alone and they were usually mined on his behalf by procurators who used slaves for labour with the assistance of military detachments.

These examples, and particularly the one bearing the II legion's name, show that the imperial administration of Britain was keen to exploit sources of metals as quickly as possible. They also show that local information had been gathered and the land swiftly surveyed for likely sites. One of these was probably at Charterhouse-on-Mendip, which became a long-term mining settlement with some of the features more appropriately attributable to a small town. Charterhouse is one of many lead mining settlements of Roman date in the area. A small fort here almost certainly belongs to the initial phase of mining. Samian found on the site indicates that it belongs to the years before about 75. The fort would have housed a small garrison, perhaps of soldiers from the II legion, detached to guard the site and oversee slave labour. However, it is quite probable that a military presence was not permanent and the settlement may have become completely civilian, but perhaps under control of civilian administrators.

Lead was also extracted in the north. A unit called the *cohors* II *Nerviorum* was based some 16km (10 miles) south of Hadrian's Wall at Whitley Castle, Alston. Its soldiers seem to

have been involved in extracting lead during the third century from a known nearby source. The lead was packaged and secured with seals stamped for the unit bearing its name and the word '*Metal[lum]*'. A number of the seals (about 133) have been found at Brough-under-Stainmore to the south where there was a fort. So it seems that the metal was being transported southwards overland either just to York, or perhaps further by sea. Lead was an extremely important metal in the ancient world, used mainly for piping and waterproofing. Mixed with tin it was used to make pewter tableware which became popular in Britain in the third and fourth centuries (**28**). It was also used with copper and tin to make bronze.

The main sources of iron in Britain during Roman times were conveniently close to the most settled area, for example in the Forest of Dean (Gloucestershire) and the Weald of Kent and East Sussex. Although not part of the highland zone there is evidence for mining and smelting being under military supervision. Recent survey work in the wetlands around the Severn Estuary has shown that land reclamation works, for example at Rumney Great Wharf, were apparently connected with the smelting of iron, evidenced by slag and iron scrap. The ore had probably come from sources in the Forest of Dean, for example Lydney, a former Iron Age hillfort which is known to have had an iron mine in the late Iron Age and early Roman period (see **92**). There is no specific evidence for military involvement here but it is likely given the location, close to the legionary fortress at Caerleon. Iron is also found in a number of deposits in the Weald, which was also thickly forested in ancient times, an ideal source of fuel in the form of charcoal. Iron was already being smelted out of the ore in this area before the Roman Conquest but on a very small scale. At places like Beauport Park (East Sussex), Roman mining and smelting began to

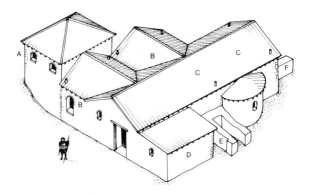

28 *Pewter jug from Appleshaw (Hampshire). It formed part of a hoard of pewter tableware recovered from close to the site of a Roman house, and would have been made from lead and tin mined in Roman Britain. Fourth century.* (British Museum.)

29 a *Reconstructed isometric view of the bath-house at the ironworking site at Beauport Park (East Sussex). A changing room; B warm rooms; C hot rooms; D cold bath; E disused furnace; F furnace.*
b *Tile from the bath-house at Beauport Park bearing the impression of a tile comb, and an official stamp. The tile comb (used to create a textured surface for bonding; see also* **69** *and* **79***) and the stamp carried the initials* 'CL BR' *for the* Classis Britannica, *the Roman fleet in Britain which seems to have been in charge of operating the mineworks.*

take place very early in the province's history but it was not until the second century that major widespread development took place.

Beauport Park is one of a number of Wealden sites that have produced evidence for the presence of the fleet, the *Classis Britannica*, in this case a remarkably well-preserved bath-house buried by a slag heap which probably subsided during the third century. Many of the tiles used in the bath-house's construction were stamped with the fleet's abbreviated title, 'CL.BR' (**29**). However, artefacts from the bath-house, which include coins and samian, point to a mid-second-century date for the building's construction, so it is probable that major development did not take place until then. The bath-house forms

only a tiny part of a sprawling mining complex.

The fleet's role in iron extraction is a little difficult to understand but the sources of iron were close to the fleet's bases at, for example, Dover and Lympne, and it may have been considered an expedient arrangement considering that much of the army was stationed so far to the north and west. Moreover, the iron may have been exported to the Continent, and the fleet's usefulness for this is obvious, especially considering that the coast line of Sussex was very different in the Roman period. Bodiam, to the north of Beauport Park, lay at the end of a large inland harbour and this convenient access into the heart of the Weald helps further explain the role of the fleet in extracting iron. Production dwindled during the third century and the iron seems generally to have been worked out (from a Roman point of view) by the fourth.

The remains of most Roman mining activities are confined to either the finished product or waste materials, such as slag. Beauport Park is still littered with fragments of slag to this day. During the Victorian period the Roman slagheap was used as a convenient source of clinker for railway tracks. Occasionally it is possible to identify some of the actual workings. At Dolaucothi in west Wales a substantial complex of aqueducts, leats, sluices, open-cast and shaft mines was developed to extract gold. Some of these can still be seen today. The technology was sophisticated and organized. A series of wooden water-wheels was used to raise water out of the deeper shafts in order to keep them drained. The mining was supervised from a fort on the site known as *Luentinum* and a road link led eastwards across southern Wales to the first-century legionary fortress at Usk, and subsequently Caerleon. Wales was a rich source of other metals, for example lead (see above p.43), iron, copper and zinc.

Metal extraction, while important, did not actually take up a great deal of land. Most of the native population in the military zone would have had little to do with it, unless they were forced to labour in the mines. This was a common punishment for prisoners. For the rest of the population agriculture would have been the primary activity.

Villas in the military zone

In chapter 2 it was shown that in the central and southern parts of Britain although native farmsteads remained in use many were gradually replaced with rectangular houses, and villas, even modest ones, proliferated in several areas. By the end of the second century even comparatively underdeveloped places like the Catsgore village or Fenland settlements had seen the benefit of improved living standards. In the military zone this was far less common. This reflected the marginal nature of much of the land, the lack of urban demand and pos-

sibly the restricting presence of the army. It may also reflect the lack of archaeological exploration to some degree but this is becoming less significant as advances in aerial surveying techniques produce more results.

Even so the army needed to be fed and naturally there would have been some convenience in obtaining food locally. During the first and second centuries a great deal of pottery was moved into the military zone in the north from sources in Dorset and around the Thames Estuary. Known as 'Black-Burnished ware' by archaeologists, the pottery consisted of a number of basic utilitarian designs of coarse jars, bowls and dishes (see **81**). The net value of the items was probably very low and they could easily have been made closer to the forts. It has been argued that it made economic nonsense to ship such low value goods over long distances and that therefore the pottery was only an incidental part of consignments which were made up largely of food. Of course there is virtually no evidence for the transport of food, but the fort at South Shields, which lies on the south bank of the Tyne Estuary, played an important role in Septimius Severus' Scottish campaign in the early third century. A large part of the fort was given over to granaries which stored grain almost certainly shipped up the east coast of Britain. This would have been an elaboration of existing arrangements, so we can imagine that the northern garrisons were supplied extensively from the south by sea, indirectly testified by the appearance of the coarse pottery, and only supplemented locally.

The northern part of Britain, and Wales were less suited to arable farming though it was established in some areas. Ploughing is harder on hillsides where soils are thinner and crops are more exposed. The general result is that yields for a given area are likely to be lower than in the southern and eastern part of the island. This suggests that arable farming in the highland zone was unlikely to produce much in the way of a surplus even if it was productive enough to support a local farming population. However, some places were fertile enough to permit the belated development of a few villas, particularly in eastern Yorkshire, though field systems show that arable farming was more widely distributed than villas, for example in Cumbria. At Dinorben in north Wales a disused hillfort was occupied by a round house during the third and fourth centuries. Despite the

45

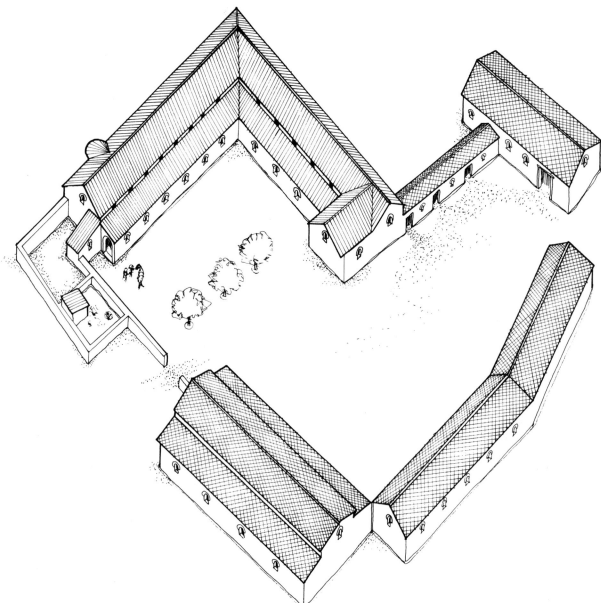

30 *Reconstructed axonometric view of the remote villa site at Llantwit Major (Glamorgan). Note the main villa house at upper left connected to a range of outbuildings facing another range of buildings in the foreground. The nearer range includes an aisled building, perhaps used to house farm workers.*

primitive housing the site yielded an iron plough-share.

The villas which did develop evidently be-longed to people who had similar aspirations to their more sophisticated counterparts in the civilian zone. The villa at Rudston (East York-shire) had several fourth-century mosaics including a bizarrely primitive portrayal of Venus. The figure owes more to Celtic tradi-tion, with its inclusion of the vulva and exag-gerated hips, than it does to classical tradition. The house also had a better executed floor which depicted a charioteer, the Four Seasons, and four birds, though even this looks clumsy compared to southern examples. Nevertheless the floors show that the owner had reached a point where he had money to spare on luxuries.

In south Wales the villa at Llantwit Major was a rare case of a long-established household (**30**). The stone house seems to date back to the second century, though there may have been a farm on the site even before that. Despite this, the site was possibly abandoned during the third century but was reoccupied in the fourth. The house and its outbuildings received a number of additions, creating a semi-enclosed courtyard. The subsequent demolition of the 'villa house' along with the maintenance of the more utilitarian buildings suggests that either it was the centre of a slave-run establishment, or that the owner was unable to afford the upkeep of non-functional buildings. If it was slave-run the farm would now have been managed by a bailiff or tenant on behalf of an absentee landlord. Of course we have no idea who the owner was but we could speculate that he might have been a *civitas* official or retired soldier who lived at Caerwent. It was quite normal practice for wealthy people in the Roman world to own villas which were actually run by tenants or bailiffs but the lack of villas in the highland zone shows that it was not a popular area for buying or developing rural estates.

One of the few sites in Wales which has been excavated in recent years is at Whitton (Glamorgan). Occupied throughout the Roman period Whitton started life as a native settlement but developed into a villa. This was common further east but very unusual for Wales. During the first century several timber round houses occupied a ditched enclosure. In the second century these were replaced with at least four separate rectangular stone buildings, but the original enclosure was retained. Although it was not as elaborate as Llantwit Major, Whitton was nevertheless still unusual for the area. The retention of the enclosure indicates an adherence to tradition, which is what might be expected if ownership of the site had remained in the same family.

Native settlements
Although little is known about prehistoric settlement in Cumbria new evidence from aerial photography and surveying suggests that farming settlements were much more common in the Roman period than previously thought. The low-lying land on the south side of the Solway Firth was particularly popular. The area lies close to Hadrian's Wall and a number

of other forts were sited in the area, for example Maryport, Ravenglass and Old Carlisle. The location of the forts may even reflect the proximity of productive land as well as strategic considerations. However, the west coast of Britain is both longer and less easily navigable than the east coast so this may have placed more importance on local supplies of food to fort garrisons.

The forts had civilian settlements attached to them. Writing tablets from Vindolanda, a military site near Hadrian's Wall, contain numerous references to foodstuffs, most of which could have been supplied locally. These include various meats, dairy products and grain. The sources of food transported to the Cumbrian and Wall forts would have included the numerous Cumbrian farming settlements which have been identified from aerial photography. Typically these consisted of enclosures with associated field systems, with a bias to the better land rather than clustering around forts or land alongside roads. However, this did not apparently restrict access as many of the settlements appear to be linked by trackways. Unfortunately evidence for the type of farming is restricted to a few quernstones, though the various field systems include those suited to arable farming and stock enclosures for pastoral farming. The latter is certainly testified in Scotland by Cassius Dio. The soldiers stationed at the forts also supplemented their food supplies by hunting. An altar from Weardale in County Durham was probably erected by a soldier who hunted in the area (**31**).

Similar settlements have been identified on the other side of the Pennines in Northumberland, well to the north of Hadrian's Wall. Field systems have been discovered which seem to have settlements as focal points, for example at Brands Hill North, some 55km (33 miles) north of the Wall, where five settlements lay close to one another. They were linked at least in part by walled trackways so we can imagine a close-knit community of probably related families. Like the Cumbrian settlements there is minimal evidence for actual agriculture but what there is points to mixed farming. Pollen evidence from the north-east, including areas south of the Wall, suggests a long period of extensive forest clearance and the appearance of cereals. At Grassington (West Yorkshire) an extensive field system can still be seen on the ground with banks defining the borders of the

31 *Altar from Weardale (Durham), dedicated to Silvanus, a woodland god, by Aurelius Quirinius who was probably a soldier from the nearby fort at Bowes.*

it likely that they were being used for stock enclosures. However, the general impression gained from all the Northumbrian evidence is that farming expanded during the Roman period, possibly because of demand from the army.

Very few of these sites have been excavated so there is little evidence for the degree of romanization which had taken place (in some cases even the Roman date is questionable). Nevertheless the structures in these farming settlements never developed into anything which might be described as a villa house. There was access to Roman trading systems, probably via fort *vici*, where samian pottery and manufactured metal goods were bought. Despite this modest level of development there was a move away from the traditional round house, just as further south at a generally much earlier date. At Penrith a round house was in use during the second century within a circular ditched enclosure. By the third century it had been replaced by three rectangular structures but these were hardly proto-villas (**32**). They had stone floors but their walls were timber. There may have been internal divisions but like other examples which have been found these buildings were nothing more than a rectangular version of their predecessors. At Ewe Close, also in Cumbria, earthworks still visible seem to represent several round houses and various enclosures all grouped together. The whole resembles a small village and lay just beside the main western Roman road running north to Carlisle. Like Penrith it was very modest. If the Roman army was providing an economic stimulus by creating demand it was obviously only to a limited degree.

In Wales native settlements have been identified in most areas except for the western part of the central zone. They were most concentrated in the north, particularly the north-west, and the south-west. The north-western settlements were characterized by stone houses (round or rectangular) built into stone enclosures and associated with field systems. There were two forts of significance in the area at Caernarfon (*Segontium*) and Caerhun (*Kanovium*). These, with their *vici*, would have acted as sources of demand for agricultural produce. Evidence for agriculture is once again circumstantial rather than specific but field divisions in terraced units, plus a quernstone from a farmstead at Cae'r Mynydd certainly point to

individual fields. Under some Roman military sites plough-marks have been identified but these merely indicate that ploughing was taking place at some time *before* the location was taken over by the army. On the other hand uncleared stones from some field systems make

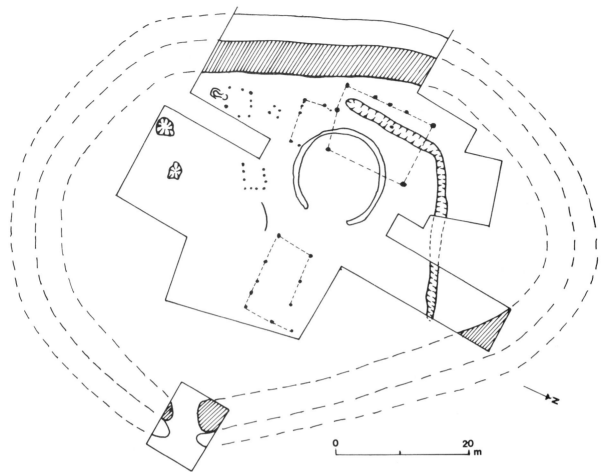

0   20
|_____|_____| m

32 *Plan of the native settlement at Crossfield Farm, Penrith (Cumbria). The enclosure contained a number of rectangular structures and an earlier round house.* (After Higham and Jones.)

arable. Sites identified in the south-west, such as Cwmbrwyn, have been less certainly associated with agriculture altogether. Only in isolated instances did any of these sites develop into villas, such as Whitton.

The quotation from Adam Smith at the beginning of this chapter shows that in the eighteenth century the highland area was largely regarded as a source of animal produce for the rest of the island. Climatic changes and the demands of the Roman army aside, we need to bear this in mind and consider whether it was a factor in Roman Britain. It may be that much effort was put into pastoral farming as a main way of earning money, while arable farming was primarily subsistence. In 1794 a report for the Board of Agriculture on Cardiganshire in Wales stated that Welsh farmers lived on 'barley bread and potatoes, and sometimes a few herrings in the autumn when they are moderately cheap...Malt liquor and meat are not within their reach.' Potatoes were obviously not available in Roman Britain but the image of a very basic diet is clear. Yet at the time Welsh drovers are testified to have driven cattle right across the country to be sold at market in the towns. The walk from North Wales to Kent took approximately three weeks, and a trip to the Midlands a little over two weeks. Barley and corn cannot carry themselves and therefore the cattle droving made sense. So although the farming communities may have operated both pastoral and arable farming it is very possible that they only actually enjoyed the fruits of the latter while their cattle earned their tax money. Moreover the returning drovers, rather than itinerant traders, may have been the sources of manufactured goods

49

33 *Altar to Coventina, a Celtic water goddess, from a well just outside the fort at Carrawburgh on Hadrian's Wall. The altar was dedicated by the commander, Titus D . . . . Cosconianus, of the unit stationed at the fort, perhaps out of respect to local considerations. Early third century.*

34 *Altar found close to the fort at Lanchester (Durham), dedicated to Garmangabis by the soldiers from the fort about the year 240.*

further emphasizing the isolation from mainstream provincial society.

The principal problem with all these relatively remote sites is that very few have been explored in any detail. Even fewer have been comprehensively published and the very small number of datable artefacts of any kind means it is extremely difficult to be sure whether structures are contemporary with enclosures and what sort of activities formed the economic base of a site. The lack of Roman material demonstrates that these settlements functioned on the lowest rungs of the ladder of romanization. Whereas the southern and central part of the province had developed to the extent that many rural settlements now had stone houses with tiled roofs and access to large numbers of

35 *Reconstructed view of the native village at Chysauster (Cornwall).* (Painting by Judith Dobie; English Heritage.)

manufactured goods, the north and west had not. More significantly they never did.

This must reflect local conditions though it would not be fair to blame the presence of the army entirely. We simply do not, and cannot, know enough about the relationship between the army and the local population. The dedication of altars to deities which were almost certainly well-established local Celtic cults indicates a certain amount of cultural respect, and even merging, for example the well dedicated to Coventina at Carrawburgh on Hadrian's Wall (**33**). Some units brought their own gods with them, like Garmangabis at Lanchester, though the altar was erected in a quiet spot some way from the fort suggesting a link with another local deity (**34**).

In the south-west peninsula there were very few forts, such as Nanstallon in Cornwall. These were only temporary and the area was never a military zone. But beyond Exeter romanized rural settlements are virtually unknown. Instead remote fortified villages like

Chysauster served as homes for the inhabitants. The site consisted of about nine stone-built houses (**35, 36**). Each had an open courtyard with out-houses, perhaps for cattle or storage, and a circular hut which had a thatched roof supported by a timber beam set into the middle of the stone floor. A field system associated with the site shows that this was an agricultural community, almost certainly engaged in mixed farming. The site seems to have been occupied from the first century BC right through to the beginning of the fourth, with little or no discernible change along the way. Sheer difficulty of communications, added to the natural conservatism of remote rural areas are almost certainly among the main reasons for the lack of any significant social and economic development.

It is difficult to avoid the conclusion that the most significant disadvantages native settlements had in the military zone were the distances which separated them from towns and the relatively marginal land which they farmed. The word 'relatively' is important. The land was quite good enough to live off but it was not as good as the land elsewhere. In other words it was more of struggle to produce a

51

36 *View of the remains at the native village, Chysauster.* (English Heritage.)

surplus, and there were very few nearby urban markets for surplus food. The additional transportation costs which would have been incurred in moving the food great distances would not only have made it less competitive but would also have made manufactured goods both scarcer and more expensive.

In every economic sense then it would appear that remote native settlements were handicapped – a circular situation in which the lack of earning power limited the possibility of investment, thereby perpetuating the lack of earning power. This continued to be the case, as we have seen, up until early modern times. The presence of the army may in fact have helped encourage what there was, rather than inhibit it, because as we have seen, large-scale land clearances in some areas only seem to have begun during the Roman period. The army also provided the only accessible markets but the development of the *vici* around the forts, some of which have been shown to have had their own field systems and terracing, made that market a diminishing rather than increasing one. With the intermittent withdrawal of troops from the north in the late fourth and early fifth century this could only have become worse, encouraging a retreat to a more subsistence level. In Wales substantial withdrawals had taken place much earlier, mostly by the end of the second century.

Unlike the southern part of Britain the areas controlled by the military did not change significantly during the Roman period. This may partly be an archaeological perspective because the artefacts are not found in sufficient quantities to characterize the different phases. Nevertheless we can only use the archaeological evidence and we simply do not find in the military area the kind of, or at least quantity of, rural development found in the south. In the third and fourth centuries the great rural estates in the south made up for their relatively leisurely rate of development and in a number of cases exhibited signs of unprecedented levels of private wealth based on landed property.

4

The third and fourth centuries

During the latter part of the third century and throughout most of the fourth Roman Britain came of age. Insulated from most of the political and military disorders prevailing on the Continent the province seems to have been both stable and economically productive. This is reflected in the growth of the great country villas which are the most conspicuous product of the surplus wealth being created, and the development of large-scale rural industries. Even the short rebellion led by Carausius and his duplicitous successor Allectus between 286 and 296 is indicative of Britain's ability to stand on its own as a part of the Roman world.

The various military campaigns which took place during the first and second centuries in Britain attracted the attention of classical historians. The writings of Tacitus in particular, and to a lesser extent those of Cassius Dio, provide us with a historical framework for events in Britain. Occasional references in the works of other writers provide supplementary information. For most of the third and fourth centuries we have even less factual information and it is worth being aware of what this means for archaeologists.

By the early part of the third century the northern frontier had become stabilized and official attention was diverted away from Britain. Imperial rule was becoming increasingly unstable and it became almost routine for emperors to be murdered and replaced by usurpers, sponsored by a section of the army. For example Philip I (244–9) was responsible for arranging the murder of his predecessor Gordian III (238–44). He was himself killed at the Battle of Verona by Trajan Decius who had originally been sent by Philip to quell a rebellion led by one Pacatian; unfortunately for Philip, Decius decided to side with Pacatian's troops. Decius was killed in 251 during a battle with the Goths, one event in an increasingly disastrous series of incursions across the frontiers by the Germanic tribes.

These episodes, though not unprecedented, were becoming typical and in this context of sustained disorder it is hardly surprising that Britain and Gaul slipped quietly out of official control during the reign of Gallienus (253–68). Postumus, military commander of the legions on the Rhine, ruled Britain and Gaul from 259–68 quite successfully. Not only did he keep the Rhine frontier under control but there is also no indication that his usurpation was unpopular. He was succeeded by Victorinus (268–70) and Tetricus (270–73) but in 273 the 'Gallic Empire' was recovered by the official emperor Aurelian (270–75).

From the Romano-British point of view this experience may have been a powerful one. The countryside of the province had become sufficiently well developed to allow the significant improvement of rural estates. The towns had all been built up to the extent that public building and facilities were well established. There may have been a sense that Britain could well do without participating in the episodic violence and instability that prevailed across and in the Channel. Though unaffected by the incursions that did cross the Rhine Britain was not immune to sea-borne pirates from northern Europe who plagued both shipping and communications in the North Sea and the coastal settlements. This almost certainly lay behind a long-term strategy of building a series of forts along the east and southern coast of Britain, and on the northern coast of Gaul. The main period of building seems to have been

37 *The south-west gate of the Saxon Shore fort at Pevensey Castle (East Sussex), built in the mid-fourth century.*

between about 260 and 300, and the remains of some of these forts, such as Pevensey (**37**), Portchester and Richborough, are still imposing today. They may have provided a useful sense of security to dispersed rural settlements in southern Britain whose inhabitants felt threatened.

The forts were not the only measures undertaken. In the 280s Carausius was commissioned to command the fleet based in Britain and Gaul and clear the pirates. He achieved this, and so successfully that he became a popular hero, a reputation he was happy to exploit by following Postumus' example, and established himself as an independent emperor in 286. He did so easily and despite the attempts of official sources to 'rubbish' him there is no real indication that he was faced with much resistance. He issued improved coinage, much of which was struck with legends designed to emphasize the stabilizing and calming influence of his power. '*Pax*' (peace), '*Felicitas*' (happiness), '*Hilaritas*' (rejoicing), '*Laetitia*' (joy) – all stock themes but they may have had a ring of truth.

Whether we can link this episode with what can be seen in the countryside is another matter. The truth is that there is no direct link but it may be that the psychology which led to Carausius' successful rule was also behind the confidence exhibited in the villas – and it is the villas which define third- and fourth-century Roman Britain from our point of view. If Britain had not been self-sufficient then such a revolt would have been impossible to begin with. Even though enormous numbers of rural settlements have been identified from this period, far more than were once believed to exist (and it has become popular to by-pass villas in favour of researching the distribution of such settlements) the fact is that the great villas exhibit the strongest degree of identifiable change in the archaeological record. And that change is in the form of confidence, maturity, stability and productivity.

Ultimately Carausius failed. He was murdered in 293 by his associate Allectus, who was himself killed by the Roman army which arrived in 296 to recover the province. The expressed purpose of that recovery was Britain's wealth and productivity. Britain was restored to imperial control at a time of improved stability in Rome. The reforms of

38 *The Windrush Valley in Gloucestershire, looking south across a fourth-century villa site. The valley's appearance has probably changed little since the Roman period and has remained important agricultural land, as well as a desirable place to live.*

Diocletian (284–305) included transforming the administration of the Empire by splitting it into two, and breaking up provinces into even smaller units. Britain, divided into two during the reign of Septimius Severus (193–211), was now made up of four provinces, ruled probably from London, Cirencester, Lincoln and York. This may have enhanced local stability but we cannot directly link such a political change to the archaeology of the countryside. The Houses of Constantine and Valentinian produced most of the emperors of the fourth century. Although occasional usurpations still took place the chronic disorder typical of the third century had been largely suspended until the latter years of the fourth century.

The villas
The second half of the Roman period in Britain, particularly the fourth century, is often seen as the golden age of the great country villas. The valley of the Windrush in Gloucestershire and

Oxfordshire was one of the areas which was lined with Roman settlements, including villas and villages, at this time. Fertile, beautiful, close to the major town at Cirencester, and linked by water and road to London it was an advantageous location in every respect (**38**). The word *villa* was normally used by ancient writers to refer to a well-appointed country farmhouse. In a Romano-British context it is normally applied to any country house which exhibits some sort of pretension in form and content, for example the use of stone for wall footings, a plan based on right angles containing a number of distinct rooms and corridors, the possession of tessellated or mosaic floors, painted wall-plaster and perhaps a bath-suite. The number of houses which could boast some of these features in the Romano-British countryside increased considerably during the third and fourth centuries, though most did so only on a small scale.

For modern travellers with an interest in Roman Britain, however, the much larger villas like Chedworth and Bignor figure high in a list of places to visit. Their fourth-century mosaics and bath-suites reinforce the view that the Roman countryside had become a mannered place to which polite Romano-British society had retreated in order to live in luxurious comfort. Even modest Lullingstone's

39 *Fragment of wall-plaster from the villa at Hucclecote (Gloucestershire). It seems to bear a scratched representation of a house facade.* (British Museum.)

principal attractions are its single mosaic and Christian wall-paintings, both of which belong to the second half of the fourth century. By contrast the number of villas known to have had mosaic floors in the second century is still less than ten. The poor state of most remains of villas in Britain gives us little certain idea of their original appearance, though a scratched drawing on wall-plaster from Hucclecote (Gloucestershire) may be a representation of part of the house (**39**), and recent excavations of collapsed walling at Stanwick (see **52**) and Meonstoke have produced useful clues.

To some extent this impression of widespread luxury is a true one. Some houses which had been modest and comfortable in the second century were transformed by the fourth century. Bignor, for example, had been enlarged to a very considerable extent, though the third-century house which formed the basis of the building was still a visible, if half-submerged, component (**40**). There had been timber buildings of sorts at the site since the end of the first century but it is interesting that even by about 250 they had only been replaced with an unprepossessing rectangular house. Over the next fifty years it was embellished with wing-rooms in a style now described as the winged-corridor house. A common design, the winged-corridor

house was simple and functional as well as presenting a pleasing symmetrical facade, though there are a number of ways of reconstructing the form. Some houses never developed beyond this form, but those that did usually had their wings extended to surround a courtyard, with eventually a fourth wing added enclosing it.

In a small number of instances, such as Woodchester, the wings were further extended to enclose another courtyard. This is often presented in textbooks as a typological series, but this obscures the obvious fact that there was little alternative to extending the house with wings at approximate right-angles. Extending a house in a single line would have made one end ridiculously far from the other. Widening the house would have created complications with lighting internal rooms and roofing wide spans. Neither problem was insoluble but remedies were structurally complex and expensive. On the villa sites land availability was not generally a problem and therefore the simplest solution was sensible structural extension which was also the most visually appealing.

So Bignor greeted the fourth century in winged-corridor form. During the next few decades it was transformed, firstly by extending the wings, one with a bath-suite (**41**), and then by adding a barn. Subsequently the barn was demolished, the courtyard enclosed with a fourth wing, various other buildings erected and an enclosure wall built. To anyone arriving from Stane Street (the main road between London and Chichester) to the east, the villa would have presented an imposing sight on the low south-facing hill on which it sits beneath the South Downs of Sussex. This is obviously what it was supposed to do. Within the villa a series of remarkable mosaics was laid (**42** and **colour plates 6–8**), one signed tantalizingly with the letters 'TR', perhaps for Terentius, an otherwise unknown mosaicist.

The Bignor mosaics were concentrated in the north wing. The finest is the composition depicting Venus and a series of cupid gladiators in an apsidal room, probably used as a dining room. Another portrays Ganymede being carried off by an eagle to become cup-bearer on Mount Olympus. The same floor incorporates a hexagonal basin with a fountain. The walls of these rooms were embellished with painted wall-plaster. Whoever owned Bignor in the fourth century was wealthy by Romano-British

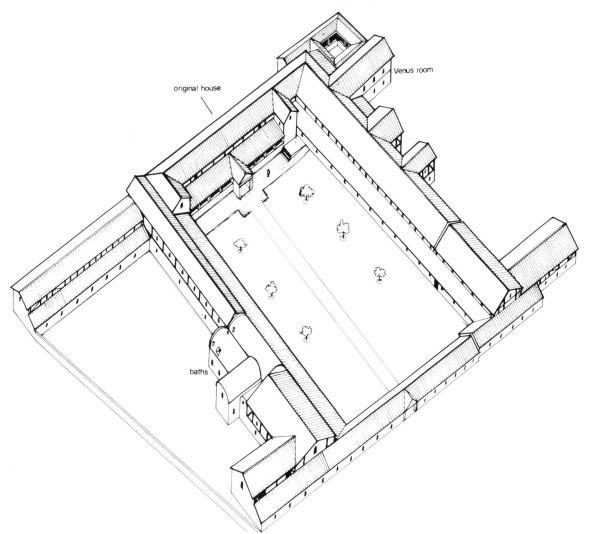

original house

Venus room

baths

40 *Reconstructed axonometric view of the house at Bignor (West Sussex), as it may have appeared in the fourth century at its height. The house had developed from a much earlier building which formed part of the later west wing. The extensions included a bath-suite and a range of rooms with an exceptional series of colourful mosaics. (See also* **41**, **42**, *and* **colour plates 6**, **7** *and* **8**.)

standards; more significantly he was obviously much wealthier than whoever owned Bignor more than a century before. Not only did he have money to spend but there were people about with whom to spend it. The most obvious are the mosaicists because their work survives, but it goes without saying that the house would

also have been equipped with some silver, and possibly gold, plate, and good quality glassware. The house was big enough to accommodate a large extended family as well as a considerable household staff.

Fine quality plate, or anything like it, is virtually never found in any sort of villa context. If the owners had left peaceably they would have taken it with them. If the house had been violated by raiders at some unspecified date then the raiders would have seized any portable goods of value. Only when such goods were hoarded and not recovered do we have a chance of seeing what may have been owned and used in wealthy rural homes. The treasure from Mildenhall in Suffolk is the finest group of silver plate known from Roman Britain. It consisted of 34 pieces, the most lavish

57

43 *Part of the hoard of fourth-century silver plate from Mildenhall (Suffolk). The large dish is 60.5cm (24in) in diameter and weighs more than 8kg (17.6lbs). Although not associated with a villa site it may be well be representative of the kind of material used in wealthy villas.*

being the Great Dish, over 60cm (24in) in diameter and weighing nearly 8.3kg (about 19lb) (**43**). Although much of the iconography on the various pieces is pagan, three silver spoons bear the Christian Chi-Rho monogram. This is of no especial significance – it was normal in Roman educated society to select features of various different cults as they suited or appealed (see Chapter 5). With no self-dating components (such as coins) the hoard can only be dated by stylistic comparison to objects of known date. On these grounds the date of deposition is thought to have been after the year 360 though many of the items could have been quite old when buried.

The Mildenhall hoard was not associated with a villa, nor does one lie in the vicinity, though a small fourth-century structure does. Although exceptional in archaeological experi-

41 *Part of the bath suite in the south wing at Bignor as it survives today.*

42 *The Venus (or Diana) mosaic from Bignor which includes various scenes from the amphitheatre (Diana was associated with the amphitheatre). Fourth century. From a drawing by Samuel Lysons. (British Museum.)*

ence it does not necessarily follow that it was exceptional for the period and it may well be that such a collection would have been paralleled in many of the great villas of fourth-century Roman Britain. As already noted there are a few very simple reasons why it would be very surprising for such items to be excavated from among the structural remains of a villa. Instead these finds are usually made by chance or at a greater distance from a site than would normally be covered by excavation. Only in recent years has the use of metal-detectors, legally and illegally, produced a significant increase in the rate of recovery. A good example of more everyday metalware was found in 1982 in the valley of the Misbourne in Buckinghamshire. The find consisted of several bronze bowls and a dish all stacked together and buried in the vicinity of a villa. Although competently made the bowls were not decorated and some had been repaired with soldering or riveted patches. They had probably seen service in the kitchen of a modest villa establishment, though it is equally possible that they had remained in use after the Roman period and had been taken from a villa. The reason for their burial is unknown. On balance it is reasonable to assume that we are very unlikely ever to have an accurate idea of the portable wealth enjoyed in rural villas.

Bignor was an important fourth-century villa but it was by no means unusual. Indeed some fourth-century houses make it look almost pedestrian. Fourth-century Chedworth, only partly excavated (**44**), was bigger and had two elaborate bath-suites (**45**) as well as a garden temple (**46**). Woodchester, excavated in the eighteenth century, has been re-examined in part and now seems to have had second-century origins. By the fourth century a steady series of alterations and additions had created a series of three courtyards (two enclosed). During the first half of the fourth century the northernmost wing was altered to incorporate the single largest room known from a Romano-British house (225 sq.m, 2400 sq.ft; significantly larger than the floor area of a Victorian semi-detached house for example) (**colour plate 1**). The square room was designed to accommodate a remarkable mosaic floor which depicted Orpheus with various animal associates in a central circular design incorporated into a series of geometric square borders. Unfortunately the floor is damaged but the

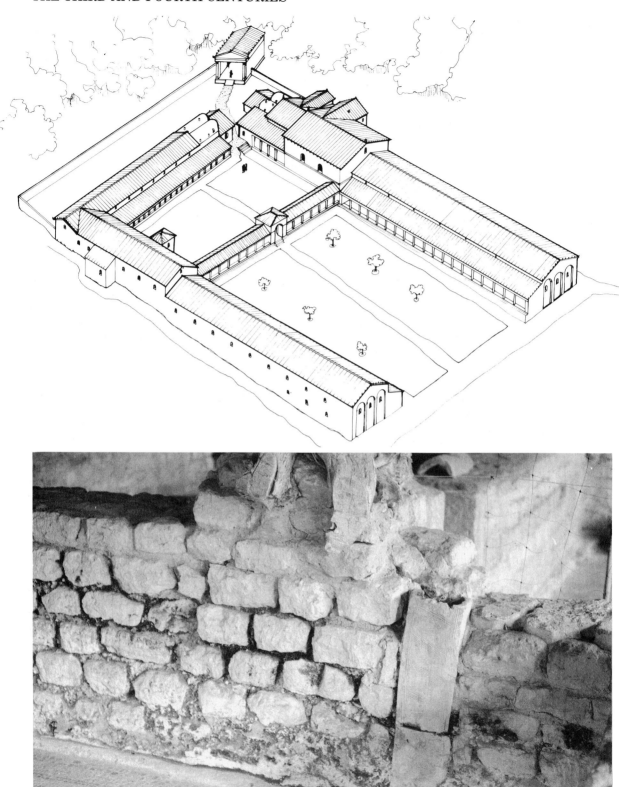

46 *Shrine or garden temple at the Chedworth villa (Gloucestershire). (See also* **44***.)*

centre is likely to have had a pool or fountain of sorts (**47**). This mosaic is one of a series of similar, though less imposing, contemporary mosaics for example that from Barton Farm close to Cirencester.

At Littlecote a mosaic floor which also may have portrayed Orpheus was laid, though unlike the others it was not laid within the house. Here a winged-corridor house had been built by the late second century. Although some structural alterations were made the house retained its basic form well into the fourth century. A nearby barn was altered out of recognition during the second half of the fourth century: the barn's roof was removed and its walls used to form an enclosure. At one end a bath-suite was built in association with a remarkable triconch hall, in which the mosaic floor was laid (**48, colour plate 2**). The triconch hall has been the subject of much debate, mostly concerned with whether it was the focal point of an Orphic cult or whether it was

44 (Left, above) *Reconstructed isometric view of the house at Chedworth. The wing in the foreground has not been fully excavated and its length is therefore assumed. Note the two bath-suites flanking the path leading up to the garden shrine in the far corner (see* **46***). (Based on views by S. Gibson but adapted and extended; see also* **colour plate 12***.)*

45 (Left, below) *Hypocaust in the west wing at Chedworth. The flue-tiles which carried hot air from the cavities beneath the floor to upper rooms (if they existed) and then up to finials can be seen cemented into a channel in the wall.*

merely an elaborate dining room. Such debates are inconclusive because the evidence does not exist to resolve them.

The Littlecote hall is certainly remarkable and was the product of a fertile imagination, but bearing in mind that the house itself was not significantly altered it is quite possible that this was a different example of fourth-century spending on villas. Here it took the form of an inspired additional building, rather than an elaboration of the existing house. Curiously the new hall was built remarkably clumsily with a number of peculiar irregularities in the plan, suggesting that it was erected in some haste. About the year 300 the whole site was 'improved' with the addition of a large stone gateway, roughly aligned on the axis of the house. It may be of relevance that the erection of the new bath-suite seems to have coincided with the removal of the older one in the house. As we have no knowledge of what decorated the hall's walls, or any ritual artefacts that may have been used in it, a case for a religious function cannot really be supported, though this does not mean it is demonstrably wrong.

There were other houses whose owners appear to have had money to spend on extravagant projects rather than simply extending their buildings. At Holcombe (Devon) a straightforward corridor house with a single wing was modified during the fourth century. An octagonal bath-suite was quite literally 'tacked on' to one end of the house. It is so out of proportion, both in terms of scale and architectural pretension, and perhaps even taste, to the rest of the building that it has been suggested that this was not a house at all, and was instead some sort of cult centre with bathing as a feature (which in archaeological cult parlance usually means healing). Unfortunately there is of course no evidence for this at all and such assertions deprive the Romano-British of the vanity of self-indulgence and outright vulgarity.

At nearby Lufton an even more preposterous octagonal bath-suite was built around the same time (**49**). Its design exceeded the abilities of its architect and required substantial buttresses to keep it up. Great Witcombe villa is a slightly more balanced version of the same sort of idea. Built during the middle of the third century and altered before *c*.300 it was intended to take advantage of a superb natural location on a hillside near Gloucester. It had to be terraced

47 *Part of the Orpheus mosaic from the villa at Woodchester (Gloucestershire) as recorded and restored by Samuel Lysons in the eighteenth century. The central octagon probably contained a fountain and pool. The column bases indicate that the ceiling was very high and they may have supported an upper gallery from where the floor could be fully appreciated.*

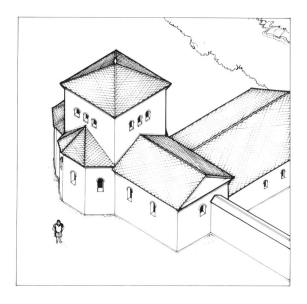

48 *Reconstructed isometric view of the triconch hall at Littlecote (Wiltshire). (See also **98** and **colour plate 2**.)*

into the slope and required buttressing to keep it there, a battle made more arduous by the presence of springs which run beneath the house. But the battle was won for its remains are still where they were supposed to be and it makes a pleasant visit to this day, especially in the summer (**50** and **colour plate 3**).

All the houses so far mentioned were the subject of a great deal of expenditure at some point during third and fourth centuries. Or at least that is what it seems – it could be that mosaics and building materials had become much cheaper, though if that were the case then we might expect such houses to be even more widespread. However, the number of villas which developed into luxurious country seats is not very great and even some of those which did, like Gadebridge Park, had been demolished long before the end of the fourth century. Rockbourne (Hampshire) lies some way from the main concentrations of villas. Although it had a history stretching back at least as far as the first century and had become quite extensive it never became a 'rich' villa. The owner had aspirations – he added hypocausts (**51**) a small bath-suite (**colour plate 9**) and a few simple mosaics in the fourth-century – but never had the means enjoyed by villa owners in better locations. At Redlands Farm, Stanwick, the simple house had nothing more than a small pair of wings and a hypocaust added. At least one of the wings proved structurally unsound and had to be pulled down.

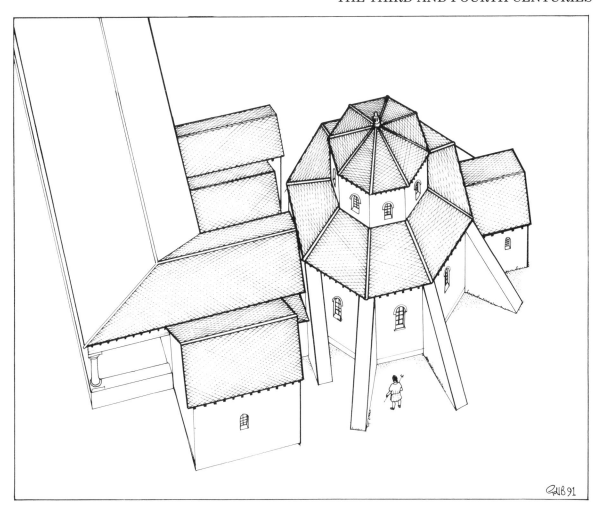

49 *Reconstructed axonometric view of the house at Lufton (Somerset), showing the bath-suite with its remarkable octagonal* frigidarium.

This fiasco had archaeological benefits for much of the pulled-down walling was left where it fell, allowing an unusually detailed reconstruction drawing to be made (**52**). This straightforward house was probably typical of many Romano-British farmhouses which have normally attracted little attention.

At some sites two or more houses seem to have been 'joined' up to make a single larger complex. Sometimes the components are readily visible from the ground plan. At Sparsholt (Hampshire) a simple aisled house of second-century date was adapted around the beginning of the third century to include inter-nal divisions and a bath-suite. It was accompanied by a new winged-corridor house and a barn-like structure on two other sides of a rectangular enclosure which was built to join them all up. The new winged-corridor house faced the entrance to the enclosure. At Gayton Thorpe (Norfolk) two winged-corridor houses were connected by a single room in 'siamese twin' style (**53**). At Mansfield Woodhouse (Nottinghamshire) a second-century winged-corridor house was joined by a fourth-century aisled house though these were not physically connected. Incidentally this is the opposite order of building types to Sparsholt which demonstrates that house type is not necessarily indicative of date. Chedworth may have been formed from three individual houses.

A particularly interesting example of an enlarged villa site was excavated at Norton

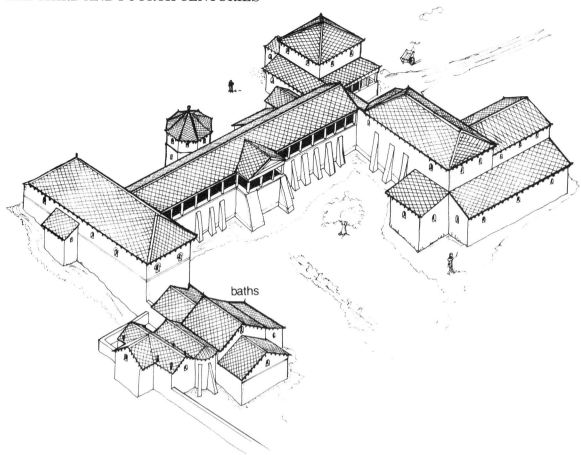

baths

Disney (Lincolnshire) during the 1930s (**54**). Well beyond the main concentrations of villas in the central and southern part of the province, Norton Disney was a modest affair insofar as domestic facilities were concerned. The site appears to have had its origins back in the first century and until the beginning of the third consisted almost entirely of timber structures. Some time between about 200 and 230 a pair of buildings was erected in stone. The smaller, probably the actual residence had three or four rooms, two with mosaic floors, and a flanking corridor. At right angles to it was a more complicated basilican-type or 'aisled' house with a distinct entrance at one end. During the third century the smaller house seems to have had a tower added to it. At about this time the houses were surrounded by a network of ditches. Although these create the impression that the house was fortified it is more likely that the ditches were designed to drain the site which was made damp and marshy by a layer of clay about 2m (6½ft) below the surface.

50 *Reconstructed isometric view of the house at Great Witcombe (Gloucestershire). The bath-suite lies in the foreground. (See also* **colour plate 3**.)

51 *Hypocaust from the villa at Rockbourne (Hampshire).*

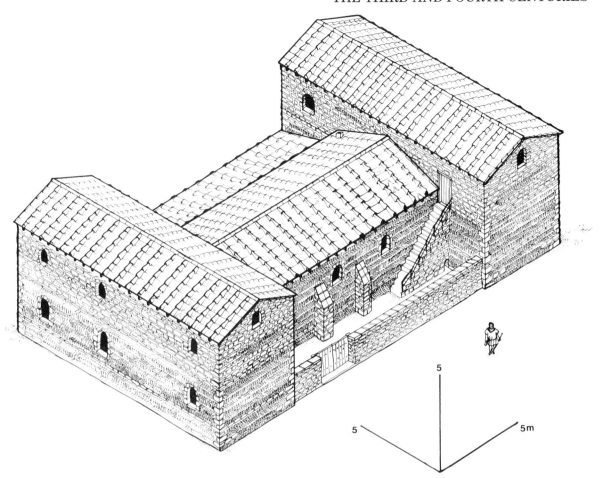

52 *Reconstructed isometric view of the house at Redlands Farm, Stanwick (Northamptonshire) based on the parts of fallen walls at the site. The courtyard in the foreground is speculative as is the external staircase. The heights of walls, however, are certain, as is the use of stone, though the building may well have been plastered or at least whitewashed.*

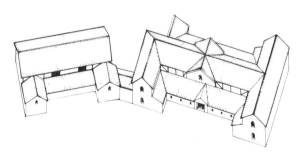

53 *Reconstructed axonometric view of the house at Gayton Thorpe (Norfolk).*

Despite the relatively small size of the buildings Norton Disney had also clearly experienced an up-turn in its fortunes at the beginning of the third century. Even a fire which caused serious damage was followed by comprehensive reconstruction. The affluence seems to have continued well into the fourth century when the 'tower' was replaced by a bath-house which also served to connect the two houses. The houses stood on a patch of high ground very close to the Fosse Way, about 15km (9 miles) south-west of the *colonia* at Lincoln and about 2.5km (1½ miles) north-east of a minor settlement at Brough, *Crococalana*. So its access to communications was excellent and the subterranean clay meant that water was readily available. As so often, it is impossible to be certain what constituted the site's economic base, but it is likely that agriculture was the main source of income. The basilican building probably accommodated much of the peripheral work associated with farming and

65

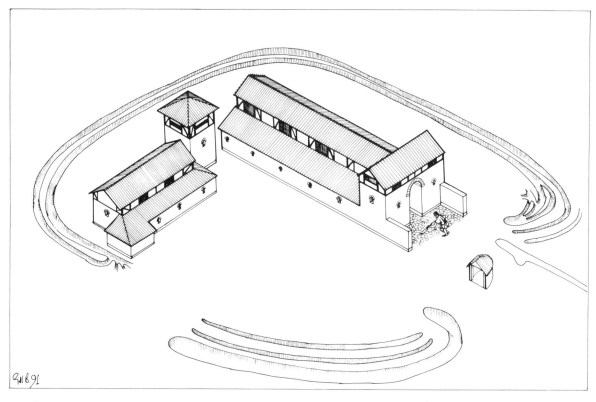

54 *Reconstructed isometric view of the house at Norton Disney (Lincolnshire). The ditches may have served as drains, rather than defences.*

also the men and families who worked there.

These various cases may represent extended families living in close proximity, certainly something which would have fitted Celtic tradition. As wealth grew, money was found for a new house for a son and his family, or alternatively to house a resident bailiff and estate workers. Where the structures were augmented to create a more cohesive whole, as at Chedworth or Rockbourne, this may represent the buying out of separate families by a single purchaser intent on providing himself with a more monumental residence. However, it is unwise to read too much into house plans and layouts. Any number of circumstances could have contributed to a single case.

The majority of 'villas', while comfortable and well-built, did not become especially elaborate, though they do show signs of significant fourth-century expenditure. During the third and fourth centuries, the average size of 'villas' diminished as the numbers increased because more people found that they now had the means to emulate the very well-off in smaller houses by installing mosaics and baths. At Barton Court Farm, the appearance of anything approximating to a villa at all was delayed until the late third century or after (**55**). Up to that point an elementary rectangular structure of sorts had been considered quite sufficient by the owners of the site at Barton; or at least that was what they had had to put up with. By the late third century a stone villa had been erected on the site. It was simple and small but it still had a corridor, an apsidal room, tessellated floors and painted wallplaster.

The house at Brixworth (Northamptonshire), is another good example of one of these bourgeois villas. Here a very unpretentious stone house had been in existence since the late first century, barely increasing its size by a half over the next two hundred years (see **17**). In the fourth century, though, money was found to build not just a corridor but also a bath-suite (**56**). The baths were never used but even so the house had been doubled in size. At Bancroft (Buckinghamshire) a timber aisled house was in use until the late second century when it was replaced with a stone winged-corridor house on

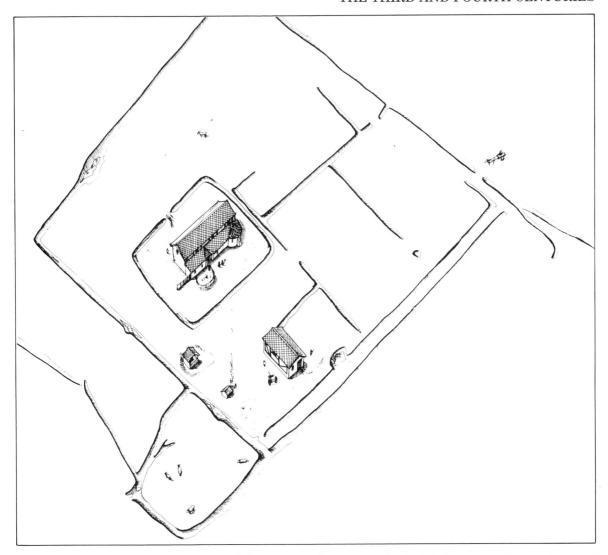

55 *Reconstructed axonometric view of the house at Barton Court Farm (Oxfordshire) as it may have appeared during the fourth century. Note the use of ditches to divide up the land around the building. (Compare with the plans on* **7**.*)*

a different alignment.

About the year 340 the house had a small bath-suite added and a number of mosaic floors laid while an ornamental garden was planted in front (**57**); however, the basic structure of the house was not altered at all.

The excavation of the site at Bancroft has revealed much about the extent and make-up of a villa estate. It is important to remember that most (but not all) villas would have only been the principal buildings on large estates of varying sizes. Extensive excavations at Stanwick (Northamptonshire) have shown the existence of a long-term site with an affluent villa, a related 'native' village and other estate buildings along with gullies and ditches used to demarcate pieces of land. The development of such estates is almost impossible to trace and identifying their full extent even more so. The almost total alteration of the English landscape following the introduction of wide-scale enclosure after 1761 has made it difficult to locate old land boundaries. Sometimes natural features such as hills make the limits likely. These have been used at Bignor to estimate agricultural land in the region of 800ha (about 2000 acres). At Ditchley some surviving features

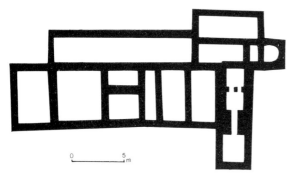

56 *Plan of the house at Brixworth (Northamptonshire), in its fourth-century form. Compare with* **17** *to see how the basic rectangular structure was extended to include a corridor and a bath-suite, though the latter was never apparently used. The house is an interesting mix of pretension and economy.* (After Turland.)

such as earthworks and woodland to the north, and the main road of Akeman Street to the south, give some idea of a possible estate. The granary's capacity has been estimated to reflect an estate of around 400ha (about 1000 acres). Other possible clues lie in old parish boundaries or medieval estates known to have been in existence at the time Domesday Book was drawn up in the eleventh century. At Withington (Gloucestershire) natural features of a self-contained valley indicate a villa estate of around 1760ha (4400 acres). By the beginning of the eighth century a new minster there had been granted through a royal endowment an estate of almost identical size, which makes it likely that the estimate of the villa estate is correct, and that it had survived.

The problem for archaeologists and historians alike is that the villas help promote a rather distorted image of fourth-century Roman Britain. Even Barton Court Farm's new house or Brixworth's extensions seem to prove that relatively poor establishments had accumulated enough capital by the later Roman period to spend it on an attempt at refined country living. Not only do villas attract more attention but they are easier to find. But in actual fact known villas form a very small proportion of the potential number of fourth-century rural sites, and therefore were probably occupied by a very small proportion of the population. This has been estimated at about 1 per cent. The principal basis for this assertion

has been the enormous increase in identified rural sites found as a result of aerial photography and fieldwork. Even allowing for the difficulty in dating unexcavated sites and therefore making an accurate estimate, it is fairly clear that even modest villas belonged to a rather limited and affluent part of the Romano-British rural population.

Villages

The general process of rural development implicit in the improved villas is also partly reflected in village sites. However, in general villages remain almost untouched by excavation and evidence for their existence is fundamentally dependent on ground and aerial observation. While these are excellent means of demonstrating the presence of a settlement they rarely produce much in the way of convincing evidence for dates. A problem is that the dating of late Roman pottery, such as Oxfordshire or New Forest products, relies on more regional associations and subjective assessments of fabric and slip. Earlier fine ware products, principally Gaulish samian, can be much more easily and convincingly associated with the work of individual and identifiable potters both through the use of distinctive designs and name-stamps. Not only that, but their products were far more widespread over western Europe and are also found on military sites which can be associated with specific, historically recorded, events. By c.240 the Gaulish samian industry had to all intents and purposes collapsed. Even coinage was prone to much more extreme fluctuations in supply. Villages, being by definition occupied at a lower standard of living, produced far less in the way of datable material at the best of times. Excavations have been so limited that it is only in a

57 *Plan of the villa estate at Bancroft (Buckinghamshire).* 1 *is the third-century winged-corridor house facing east,* 7 *is the earlier rectangular house in use up to the end of the second century when it was demolished. Note the extensive traces of ditches and gullies. The house was accompanied by an octagonal structure at* 5, *probably a garden house, and a further (utility?) building at* 8. *Buildings* 2, 3 *and* 9 *were probably barns or for storage while* 4, 11 *and* 12 *may have bee used by workers or for animals.* (After Williams.)

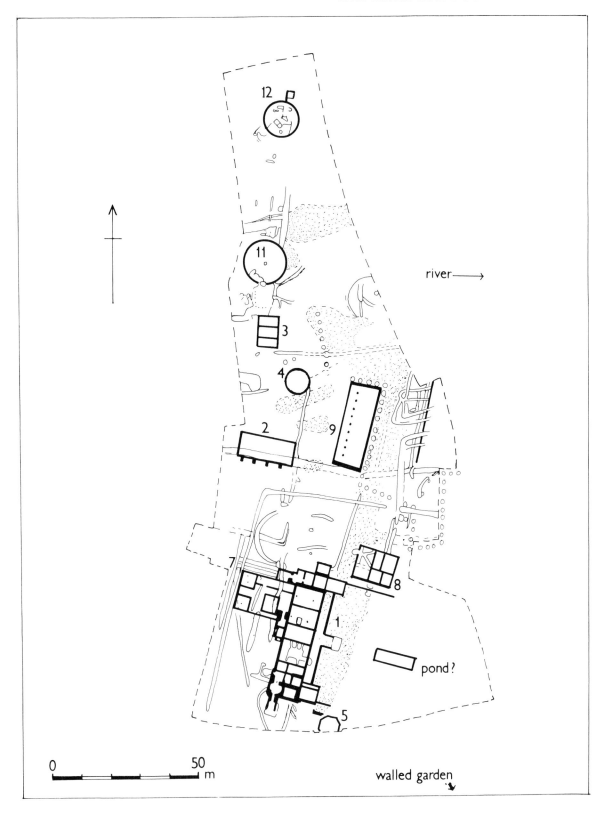

river ⟶

walled garden

pond ?

0   50
              m

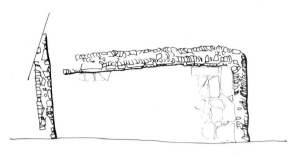

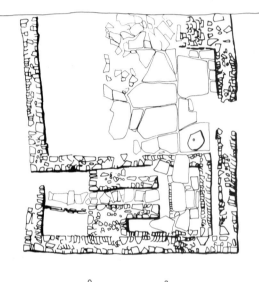

0 ___ 3 m

58 *Plan of a house (building 3.6) in the village settlement at Catsgore (Somerset).* (After Leech.)

few cases that we can observe a sequence of development throughout the Roman period.

Catsgore, already a long-established settlement, received a number of new buildings in the fourth century and had at least 12 separate farms (**58**, see also **21** and **78**). It was almost certainly associated with a nearby villa. This is important because it is likely that many of these villages housed people who worked at least in part on villa estates. Indeed the growth of villas and many villages were probably inextricably linked. Gatcombe, where the remains of the villa proper were destroyed by railway work long before excavation of the site, has been shown to have consisted of a walled area which actually contained something like a village within the villa compound. This included buildings given over to metalworking, an abbatoir and a mill. This has also been described as

a villa compound but the effect would have been the same – villas with a number of associated working and accommodation buildings amounted to being villages, in the sense that a village is a self-contained small rural community.

Similar situations have been noted elsewhere. At Kingscote (Gloucestershire) extensive surface traces of occupation around the villa point to the presence of a large number of buildings scattered in the vicinity of the house and alongside the Roman road which passes across the site. At Stanwick (Northamptonshire) the villa has now been associated with an extensive village of as yet unknown size. However, in this case most of the rectangular masonry village buildings seem to have been built in the latter part of the second century. They remained in occupation through the third and fourth centuries though some new building took place. Most of the wells located date to the fourth century so the site was evidently still thriving. Some of the village houses appear to have had timber enclosures put up around them. This may point to the conversion of slave into tenant, and therefore nominally independent, labour.

Nettleton, on the Fosse Way, is of primary archaeological interest because of its octagonal temple dedicated to Apollo (see **88** and **colour plate 14**). Ever since the temple was built there had been something of a village-like settlement. Initially there is little evidence to show that this settlement was anything other than peripheral to, and dependent on, the temple. The temple experienced partial collapse about 330 and thereafter the settlement seems to have become more involved in the manufacture of pewter, a popular alloy in the late Roman period. Made from lead and tin, pewter is a pliable substance which is easily melted down and moulded. It was therefore easily recyclable and Britain of course had deposits of both metals. It came to serve many of the functions previously fulfilled by fine-ware pottery. Most of the evidence for the manufacture of pewter vessels has been found in rural settlements. Nettleton produced fragments of moulds, as has Camerton, also in Avon, and Leswyn St Just in Cornwall. Here, then, we have a number of cases of light industrial activity going on in the countryside, rather than in the towns which was more the case in the first and second centuries.

In the Fens, at Grandford, the third and fourth centuries seem to have been a period of improvement following damage caused by flooding. The settlement was rebuilt and remained in occupation into the fourth century, but this time in stone and with buildings on different alignments. At least one had some sort of heating system. However, many settlements affected by the flooding were not re-occupied. As the evidence for agriculture in the area for the Roman period has been primarily pastoral it is likely that seeing the Fens as an enormously important source of arable production may be wrong. With settlement in decline in the latter part of the Roman period this is even more likely.

The native settlements particularly characteristic of rural settlement in the south-west, for example in Dorset, Devon and Cornwall, appear to have fallen out of use in the fourth-century. These include Chysauster and the settlements on Cranborne Chase and Salisbury Plain. Whether this was because of an official decision to clear them in order to use the land for different purposes is unknown. Alternatively it may be that the growth and success of the prosperous villa estates in the Mendips and Cotswolds had raised agricultural production to a level which marginalized the viability of an independent native settlement. It may even be, though this is completely speculative, that small-scale migrations have taken place from sites such as Woodcuts to the villa estates in search of work and better security. This would have helped contribute to the appearance of village-like settlements associated with villas.

In economic terms fourth-century Roman Britain had achieved a position where for the upper tier of society at least the possession of significant wealth had become a reality. Even though we have to remember that most of the rural population would have had little experience of cultivated villa living it is the existence of wealthy villas which separates the fourth-century countryside from the first-century BC countryside, and also the fifth-century countryside. Even at some modest sites like Catsgore there is a discernible improvement in the standard of living. The wealthy villas and the existence of rural industries with widespread markets formed a vital link in the whole economic structure of Roman Britain. The villas symbolize successful agriculture which was capable of producing a regular and reliable surplus. They were inextricably linked to the towns, which both purchased the food and supplied services and manufactured goods. The industries, like the Alice Holt potteries, point to a thriving commercial infrastructure which stretched from the towns deep into the heart of the countryside. But by the latter part of the fourth century this heady state of affairs had begun to disintegrate. This is one of the great historical enigmas of Roman Britain.

5

Rural society

Population

From an archaeological or historical perspective an ancient population is interesting from both a general (or statistical) and individual point of view. Unfortunately for Roman Britain very little is known about either. Towns have a recognizable form and, where they lie in open countryside (such as Silchester), it is possible to make at least a minimum estimate of the number of people who lived there. The identifiable buildings supply a basis and medieval towns provide parallels. In the countryside it is becoming clearer that we have only a very limited idea of the extent of settlement.

Some attempts have been made to estimate the rural population of Roman Britain. These are usually based on estimates of the urban population and derive from economic parallels with other pre-industrial societies where the ratio of agricultural communities to urban communities can be measured approximately. They range from around two to four million with a ratio to town dwellers of anywhere between fifteen and eight to one. This includes a military population, with dependants, of anything up to 200,000. The figure could have been even higher. However, we need to remember that the rural population would have fluctuated and that it is pointless to seek some sort of fixed total. We have, for example, no knowledge of disease and famine in Roman Britain. Not only that but we can be sure that some people migrated between the towns and the countryside according to the season.

Analysing the social make-up of the rural population is much more difficult, if not impossible. The great villas of the third and fourth centuries have tended to dominate archaeological thinking on rural Roman Britain largely because they provide the most to think about. The structures are the most complex and their mosaics and painted wall-plaster attract the attention of those keen to analyse and classify an otherwise largely anonymous society and economy. But the villas were occupied by the relatively wealthy and their household staff. These affluent owners belonged to a small section of the population. As new discoveries are made so that section seems to become relatively smaller as more villages and other minor rural settlements are identified.

Villa owners

The association of villas with towns reflects both social and economic factors. During the fourth century villas declined both in size and density the further away they were from major towns. This indicates that villas were not only partly an economic consequence of their proximity to towns but also that their owners had some social status in the towns. The most likely connection is that villa owners accumulated some of their wealth through occupying favourable locations close to the infrastructure of markets and trade. How they came by those estates in the first place is not discernible in any one case but it is likely that many families could have traced their origins back to aristocratic forebears before the conquest in 43.

The economic well-being of some wealthy fourth-century villa owners would have been founded in history but stimulated and sustained in the developing economy of Roman Britain. Exactly the same phenomenon has taken place in more modern times. Many major landowning families can trace the origin of their estates back to ancestors who backed the Tudor monarchs in the sixteenth century, the

Stuarts in the seventeenth or those who made fortunes out of the enormous expansion in British trade as the colonies were opened up. This should hardly surprise us as the same process is played out in all modern developing countries except in cases where a social revolution has dispossessed landowners.

Landed wealth in the Roman world served as a property qualification which entitled the head of a family to sit on a town council and to compete for the various annual magistracies. In this section of the community at least, we are almost certainly looking at families and individuals who were at ease in town and country. It might then be inferred that some of these families exploited their position in the *civitas* capitals to favour the economic advantage of their estates. Not all villa owners would have held office in a nearby town. Some residents were tenants while some owners were not even British, or resident in Britain. We know that in the year 404 a certain Melania the Younger, an exceptionally wealthy heiress, decided as part of her Christian faith to sell off a number of her estates for the benefit of the needy. She toured the Empire with her husband Pinianus disposing of estates in Italy, Sicily, North Africa, Spain, and Britain. Melania was later made a saint and it is the record of her life which contains this information (though the 'Life' of a saint was often inaccurate in detail). Melania was unusual – her wealth was considerable even by Roman senatorial standards – but her actions remind us that the Roman Empire was a cosmopolitan place where people moved about fairly freely, and could own land in several different places. While we have no idea of where her British estate was, or what it consisted of, her example demonstrates that a number of villa owners may well have lived elsewhere in the Empire, perhaps only occasionally visiting Britain.

Unfortunately our knowledge of villa owners in Roman Britain at any time is practically non-existent. One way of looking at the evidence is to try and analyse the ground-plans of the excavated houses in order to see if we can discern the number of people who lived there and how they used the space. For example there are several instances, already noted, where two separate houses were built side by side, for instance at Gayton Thorpe (see **53**). Alternatively it may be possible to identify separate groups of rooms within a single house,

such as the wings. Both may represent the presence of two families living together, either as representatives of the same extended family or possibly as two separate tenant families. However, there is a problem with this approach – a house's layout or design may have been the result of particular circumstances at only one time in its lifespan. If the circumstances altered this need not have been reflected in the house's appearance. Quite apart from that it is rare even to be certain where internal doors were located so identifying self-contained units within a house is practically impossible.

Where villa complexes consist of a number of separate buildings all contained within the same compound or area we may be looking at further examples of an extended family. Where the buildings are evidently of a quite different standard then we may be looking at a villa house occupied by the owners (or affluent tenants) and accommodation for agricultural workers. The villa at Mansfield Woodhouse (Nottinghamshire) consisted of a winged corridor house and a separate aisled building. At Llantwit Major (Glamorgan) is a more elaborate example of the same idea; here the villa house was L-shaped and looked across a courtyard to a separate aisled structure with further buildings attached (see **30**). The impression is of discrete residential and farm areas. Columella, writing in the first century, described an Italian villa estate as consisting of three main parts: the residential house, the farmhouse and the storehouse. The farmhouse, *villa rustica*, he said should contain a large kitchen area with a high roof in order to limit the risk of fire. The slave staff should live there in individual rooms, unless they worked as shepherds or herdsmen in which case they should occupy part of the buildings where the animals lived. Nevertheless, none of these buildings should be so dispersed as to hinder the foreman's ability to keep an eye on everything. This description certainly fits the appearance of a number of Romano-British villa complexes like Llantwit Major, or Winterton (Lincolnshire), even if most were far smaller than the Italian estates Columella was writing about.

Sometimes the contrast between buildings is more pronounced. The plan of the Gorhambury villa estate (**59**) (Hertfordshire) is an excellent example. Here the double compound is clearly dominated by the villa but a number of aisled structures probably represent the buildings

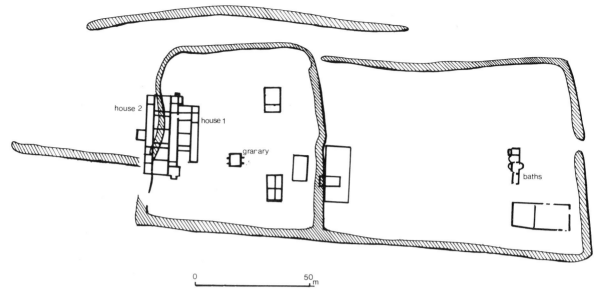

house 2

house 1

granary

baths

0   50 m

59 *Plan of the villa site at Gorhambury (Hertfordshire). (After Neal.)*

occupied by workers and animals, while an isolated bath-house is hardly likely to have been of much practical value to the villa residents. At Gatcombe (Avon) the villa house was unfortunately destroyed during nineteenth-century railway building, but a number of small buildings within the walled compound were almost certainly used for accommodation, storage and as workshops by estate workers.

Villages like Catsgore may represent more geographically dispersed examples of the same sort of arrangement, though in such cases the connection is naturally rather less easy to demonstrate. The wealthy heiress Melania, mentioned above, held an estate in Italy on which there were said to be 62 villages, each of which contained around 400 inhabitants. Again, she was exceptional in her wealth, but the practice of working estates with villages to house workers was a well-established one. The villagers and estate workers would have probably maintained a kind of deferential loyalty to the landowning family – an arrangement of mutual convenience in a paternalistic society – and this relationship could have endured through many generations, much as it did on the country estates of England in more modern times. An example is the 'Tichborne Dole', a ritual carried out by the Tichborne family in which bread was distributed to tenants on their estates in Hampshire. The event is recorded on a painting of 1670 depicting Sir Henry Tichborne in front of his house, surrounded by his household, handing bread to tenants and workers who have gathered there. Although the event was ostensibly altruistic it reinforced his duty and their dependence, and was an expression of status. The painting was carefully composed in order to leave the viewer in no doubt as to the relative importance of each individual in the microcosm of a country estate. It is obviously not an exact parallel for Roman Britain, the evidence is lacking, but it is very likely that broadly similar relationships and traditions were carried on in the villa estates. Religious ceremonies and rural temples may have been used in the same way (see below p.104).

The physical remains at many sites certainly imply the existence of a rural estate hierarchy. Occasional evidence such as iron shackles may indicate the existence of a farm worked by slaves – imperial estates were sometimes worked by slaves under the control of a procurator, though leasing out parcels of land was also normal practice. 'Slave' is an emotive word and one to which we exclusively, and understandably, attach negative associations. But it was part of Roman life and not necessarily abused in the way we interpret it. Pliny the Younger described passing evenings at his villa by walking with household staff, some of whom he refers to as educated men. Columella recommended encouraging female slaves to bear children and to exempt them from work or even free them. Of course it was possible to live in a

74

town and leave a foreman to run the estate with slaves. Even tenant farmers could do this though Columella considered such practice to be very bad form if for no other reason than that the return on land farmed in this way was usually much smaller.

The aisled houses have been mentioned several times as components of villa estates. However they also appear in many cases as individual houses, though most of these fall into fairly distinct regional groups, for example in central southern England. If they were the *villa rustica* part of a larger estate as Columella described it then perhaps they were considered suitable as farmhouses where the owners were less affluent. Alternatively they may have been built as outlying farmhouses on much larger estates which we can no longer identify. One theory is that as aisled houses resemble pre-Roman buildings known in parts of northern Europe, they may have their origins in prehistoric times. However, they are virtually unknown in pre-Roman contexts in Britain, while the practice of identifying connections through the similarities of quite simple forms is a dubious one. The aisled (or basilican) form has its own parallels in the Roman world as well.

The aisled form is essentially an extremely simple design derived from nothing more sophisticated than a rectangular one-room structure. The only difference is the division into aisle and naves by walls or pillars which increased the possible roof-span. The basic form is flexible and adaptable and this is why we find it in rural and urban contexts. At Stroud (Hampshire) the aisled house was altered by creating a number of internal rooms and adding a pair of wing rooms. The external effect was to create something which resembled a winged-corridor villa. As the main house it dominated its own villa compound. The recently discovered fourth-century aisled house at Meonstoke (Hampshire) may or may not have been part of a more extended villa compound but its elaborate facade which collapsed face-down, and has since been partially recovered, shows that it was decorated with a fair degree of architectural pretension – hardly the mark of an unimportant subsidiary house, though here, as so often, the lack of other surviving examples may award this site more individual notoriety than it would have had at the time.

The Thruxton house from which a famous mosaic was recovered (see below) was an aisled house, so clearly such buildings were not necessarily occupied by farmers of very modest means even if, as seems likely, they shared their houses with their animals. At North Warnborough (Hampshire) the distribution of artefacts within the house has been taken to indicate not just the presence of rooms given over to animals but also the segregation of male and female working areas (for example spindle whorls in one part, knives in another). Such a division would fit the context and survival of a pre-Roman Celtic family tradition of living as very large extended groups though the interpretation is perhaps a rather optimistic use of the evidence. There is no need to have to interpret all aisled houses one way or the other. As a simple and flexible design it is likely that it was used as appropriate in different contexts and this could include regional tradition as well as individual convenience.

The discussion so far has been fairly general. Being more specific about phenomena such as the aisled houses in any one case is extremely difficult because we lack the kind of evidence which would make it possible for us to understand the workings of a rural household. Even the evidence discussed above applies largely to villas, once again because they provide us with something to work from. The groups of one-room buildings in villages like Catsgore defy meaningful analysis in terms of families and individuals even if we can recognize that most of the countryside population would have lived in something like them.

Identifying individual villa owners in rural Roman Britain is practically impossible. Even the famous first-century 'palace' at Fishbourne, popularly associated with Cogidubnus, client king of the Regnenses, has yielded no evidence at all for the identity of its owner other than that he was Roman at least in his tastes and aspirations if not in actuality (see **14**). A writing tablet found recently in London records that in the year 118 during the reign of Hadrian one Lucius Iulius Betucus was engaged in a dispute in London over the ownership of a tract of land in Kent. But as so often in Roman Britain we have a very incomplete story and we do not know precisely where the land was, how Betucus came to be in a position to claim ownership and even whether a villa was involved.

75

61 *Mosaic from the house at Appleshaw, Thruxton (Hampshire), bearing the name of Quintus Natalius Natalinus.* (British Museum.)

60 *Marble bust from the 'Deep Room' at Lullingstone (Kent). Second century.* (British Museum.)

The villa at Lullingstone produced two second-century marble busts found in the 'Deep Room' where they had been deliberately hidden towards the end of the second century (**60**). Here they were occasionally visited by the people living in the house who brought libations and other gifts which indicate that the busts were regarded with some veneration. They were probably ancestor busts and the fact that they had been secreted away suggests that they had belonged to previous occupants. The busts are significant examples of competent classical sculpture, typical of the period in more affluent parts of the Empire. So it is likely that they represent members of a wealthy family, probably Gaulish or Italian in origin, who owned Lullingstone in the second century. The proximity of the house to London, and its modest size may well mean that they lived in London, perhaps engaged in provincial government, and used Lullingstone as a recreational retreat.

We cannot know any more about the people who lived at Lullingstone; indeed even the busts are exceptional. Nothing else like them has ever been found in Britain, at least in such an unequivocal association with a building. There are isolated possible instances of named owners of rural estates, but these are either not certain or cannot be associated with specific land. The *Villa Faustini* (the 'Villa of Faustinus'), named on the Antonine Itinerary, seems to have been somewhere in Norfolk or Suffolk on the road south from the *civitas* capital at Caistor-by-Norwich. The site has not been located, though a number of settlements in the area are candidates for its location. Quintus Natalius Natalinus, who named himself on a fourth-century mosaic in a villa at Thruxton (Appleshaw) in Hampshire, may have been the owner but he may equally have been a tenant (**61**). Even if he was the owner we have no idea when or how he came into ownership. He seems to have had an additional name for the inscription includes the words, '*et Bodeni*'. Bodenius is thought to be a Celtic name and indicates that he was British or Gaulish in origin, though his *tria nomina* show that he presented himself as a Roman. Apart from this instance we have nothing more than isolated graffiti like the first- or second-century silver spoon from Plaxtol

62 *Fourth-century mosaic from the house at Lullingstone (Kent), bearing an inscription referring to an event in Virgil's* Aeneid. *(See also* **colour plate 5**.)

(Kent), bearing the scratched inscription APRIL for *Aprilis*.

Classical culture and mythology

The few names discussed above indicate the existence of a 'latinized' community in which an affluent section of society aspired to mainstream Roman classical culture. This is reflected in other examples such as the Latin inscriptions from the villas at Lullingstone and Farningham. At Lullingstone the late fourth-century mosaic depicting Jupiter as the bull carrying off Europa is accompanied by a couplet which refers to both this incident and to a passage in Virgil's *Aeneid*, written nearly four hundred years earlier (**62, colour plate 5**). A wall-painting at Farningham, a short distance away, also bore a reference to Virgil. In the south-west at Frampton (Dorset) a large and complex mosaic not only contains a reference to Christianity but also includes an inscription composed in the style of the poet Ovid based on material in the *Aeneid*. Although these superficially appear to be exceptional it may well be that these inscriptions are merely rather obvious examples of a much more widespread appreciation of classical learning among the Romano-British rural well-to-do. Knowledge and appreciation of classical culture and mythology was also demonstrated by the possession of sculpture. Examples are rarely found in Britain but we can assume that in the wealthy villas at least they were probably much more common than finds suggest. From Spoonley Wood comes figure of Bacchus (**63**) and from Woodchester an elegant figure of Diana Luna (**64**).

Better evidence for classical aspirations is found in the mosaic floors with their complex iconography. It has been suggested that mosaics were largely the product of regional 'schools', based in the towns and led by a small number of master mosaicists and their apprentices. These have been discerned from the content and design of the floors. However, the mosaics associated with any one school are not very numerous and tend to be geographically

63 *Marble statue of Bacchus from a grave close to the villa at Spoonley Wood (Gloucestershire). Height about 40cm (16in).* (British Museum.)

fairly dispersed. Unfortunately we know virtually nothing about the mosaicists – only at Bignor is a floor signed, and that consists of nothing more than 'TR', possibly for an otherwise unknown Terentius (**colour plate 7**). The most conspicuous thematic group is the series attributed to the so-called Corinian Orpheus school centred on Cirencester. One is the great floor at Woodchester, which lies about 19km (11 miles) to the west (see **47**) and another is from Barton Farm, just outside the walls of the town. A distinctive feature is the presentation of animals circling in bands around the floor, and the inclusion of a figure playing a lyre, assumed to be Orpheus. Several other cases

64 *Marble statue of Diana Luna from the villa at Woodchester (Gloucestershire). Height originally about 50cm (20in).* (British Museum.)

have been located, for example at Stonesfield (Oxfordshire).

The content of the mosaic floors is very difficult to interpret. As the most aesthetically

65 *Fourth-century mosaic from Bignor (West Sussex), depicting the head of Medusa in the middle of a series of interlocking geometric forms. From a drawing made by Samuel Lysons.* (British Museum.)

pleasing and stimulating finds from villas which appear in any quantity they may attract more archaeological attention than they really deserve. Much can be made of the iconographical content which is almost invariably mythical or divine in content when figures are included (**65, 66** and **colour plate 6**). This occasionally leads to the claim that the floor is surviving evidence for the existence of cults pursued in villas, or at least practised by their owners. The Orphic floors are the most evocative in this respect and at Littlecote the combination of an Orphic floor and a triconch hall has proved one of the more favoured cases for such a cult (see **48**), as have the 'Christian' mosaics at Frampton and Hinton St Mary (Dorset) (see Chapter 7).

The recurrence of themes was just as likely to be the result of fashionable taste among a small élite group. It has been argued recently that the iconographic content of many fourth-century villa mosaics is more compatible with stock classical formulae than previously thought. In this respect the mosaics may therefore be evidence of not just classical aspirations among Romano-British villa owners but also a sound classical education as well. As such they reflect the villa owners' cultural tastes rather than being evidence of religious practices. This is an interesting and more convincing approach than the idea that every mosaic floor was designed with weighty matters of symbolism in mind. It is all too easy to forget that mosaic floors were under foot and under furniture and while important and attractive to their owners they were unlikely to be exclusive repositories of their innermost beliefs. They were part of the overall decoration of a house, which included everything needed to make it a comfortable and attractive place to live (**67**).

Social inequality in the countryside and the urban population

If villas are representative of such a restricted part of the Romano-British population how then can we account for the fact that a privileged section of the countryside's inhabitants found themselves able to spend substantial amounts of money on their homes? The answer is lost in the obscurities of the Romano-British economy and we can only speculate. It may be instructive to consider contemporary Third World cases where a number of countries have

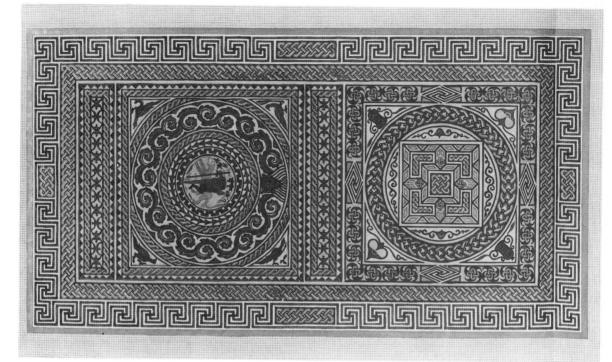

66 *Mosaic from the villa at Stonesfield (Oxfordshire), as recorded in the eighteenth century but now lost. The left-hand panel depicts Neptune, and Bacchus with a panther. Fourth century.* (British Museum.)

experienced a very considerable weakness in government power due to various destabilizing factors. As a consequence some economies have almost collapsed in spite of the possession of natural resources. But in these countries small sections of the populations have been able to accumulate substantial wealth and find ways in which to spend it on prestige and luxury 'display' goods imported from abroad.

Obviously the precise circumstances which afflict such countries are not ones which we can accurately attribute to Roman Britain, though we can bear in mind that by the fourth century the imperial government was very much weaker than it had been in the second. But these examples do demonstrate instances in which a small section live extremely well and the vast majority of the population live extremely modestly – even in dire economic circumstances, something which was apparently not the case in Roman Britain. For the wealthy the source of their capital, whether derived from exploitation, corruption, foreign

currency, or land, is effectively a self-sustaining one because no one else is in a position to challenge it. In such circumstances the majority have no access to the facilities or privileges which would guarantee them wealth.

There are various possible explanations for the increase in Roman Britain's wealthy rural class. One suggestion is that some wealthy people in Gaul opted to sell up and move to Britain, which was undoubtedly less subject to the increasing insecurity of the north-west continental provinces from the third century on. Unfortunately there is no evidence at all to confirm this, either in the literature or in the ground. Another possibility is that villa development was connected with a decline perceived (by archaeologists) in the urban population from the latter part of the second century onwards. The theory is that the ruling classes, those with the property qualifications which allowed them to sit on town councils, now embarked on a trend of moving themselves and their wealth out to the countryside but continued to sit on the councils. A statistical study has shown that, apart from London, administrative towns such as Silchester and Cirencester had more villas around them, distributed over broader areas than small towns such as Great Casterton. The decurial classes were

1 *(Right)* View of the
Woodchester villa as it
may have appeared in
its fourth-century
heyday. The large
central block housed the
Orpheus mosaic (see
47). (The Author.)

2 *(Below)* The villa and
hall at Littlecote as they
may have appeared in
the fourth century. (The
Author; see also **48** and
98.)

3   *(Above)* The hillside villa at Great Witcombe as it may have appeared in the fourth century. (The Author; see also **50** and **100**.)

4   *(Left)* A fourth-century polychrome mosaic from the villa at North Leigh (English Heritage).

5 *(Left)* Detail of the fourth-century mosaic at Lullingstone. The scene depicts Europa being abducted by Jupiter in the guise of a bull (English Heritage).

6 *(Below)* Central detail of the fourth-century mosaic depicting Medusa at the Bignor villa. (See also **65**.)

7 *(Left)* Mosaic panel from Bignor bearing the initials 'TR', possibly an abbreviation for Terentius, the mosaicist.

8 *(Below)* Detail from the fourth-century Venus mosaic at Bignor depicting a pair of cupid gladiators. (See also **42**.)

9 *(Above)* The surviving remains of the bath-suite at the Rockbourne villa.

10 *(Right)* Intaglio (gemstone) from the villa at Lullingstone. The figure is Victory, writing on a shield. Found just beside the villa with a group of second-century base-metal coins, it had been forcibly removed from its gold ring (traces of gold remained). It would have been worn by a person of high status, of interest in connection with the approximately contemporary busts (see **60**.) Length 24mm (1in). (English Heritage.)

11 *(Right)* The nymphs painted in a niche, 91cm (35in) high, in the 'Deep Room' at Lullingstone. There would originally have been three figures but damage occurred when a shelf was fitted across the middle and then subsequently the niche was filled in. Probably second century. (English Heritage.)

12 *(Below)* The villa site at Chedworth as consolidated for public display. The modern cover-buildings do not correspond to the original appearance. The view is west along the north wing. (See also **44**.)

13 The fourth-century Romano-Celtic temple on the Iron Age hillfort at Maiden Castle as it may have appeared, looking west. The small building to the left may have been a kiosk for the sale of souvenirs while the house next to the temple was probably the priest's residence. (The Author; see also **89**.)

14 View of the valley at Nettleton looking east, showing how the late third-century octagonal temple may have appeared in its heyday. (The Author; see also **88**.)

15 *(Below)* Twenty-two gold rings, part of the treasure from Thetford which included other gold and silver jewellery as well as silver spoons. Inscriptions from the spoons link the hoard with a cult of the god Faunus. (British Museum; see also **96**.)

16 *(Below)* The central part of the fourth-century mosaic from Hinton St Mary which appears to represent Christ. If so the image is a unique early picture of Christ. (British Museum.)

67 *Stone carving from Chedworth (Gloucestershire), forming part of a balustrade.*

concerned with displaying their wealth and power in order to assert and reinforce their status. Once no longer resident in the towns they spent their personal 'display budget' on large houses and fine mosaics, and were possibly also responsible for the increase in the number of rural temples.

This is a social interpretation of the evidence and it makes some sense. The main problem is that even if the urban population did decline as a result of movement away from towns, those that stayed seem to have been the relatively wealthy ones. Moreover, the decline in urban building projects may have had other reasons, the main one being that most of the necessary public buildings were completed by the beginning of the third century. There was also the possibility of investment from other parts of the Empire by people who thought Britain offered more stability; there are advantages in dispersing investments, both as a matter of security and convenience. Pliny the Younger lived in a villa on the coast during the winter, at Lauren-

tum just 27km (17 miles) from Rome, around the end of the first century. From here he easily travelled on a daily basis to the city to engage in business. In the summer he moved further inland and north to Tifernum in Tuscany, 240km (149 miles) from Rome where he owned another house. Pliny regarded this sort of policy as not only pleasurable and convenient, but also specifically described it as a sensible dispersal of his investments despite the cost of maintaining staff at each house.

The decline in villa occupation

Curiously by the second half of the fourth century there was a distinct decline in the number of villas in occupation. Fishbourne was a ruin by the fourth century; it was never rebuilt after a major fire. At Plaxtol (Kent) the second-century winged-corridor house seems to have been carefully cleared before being abandoned around the beginning of the fourth century. Over the succeeding decades it appears to have simply collapsed, quite undisturbed. Plaxtol was a small, unprepossessing house. Gadebridge Park by contrast was a considerable building in the year 350. Like so many other

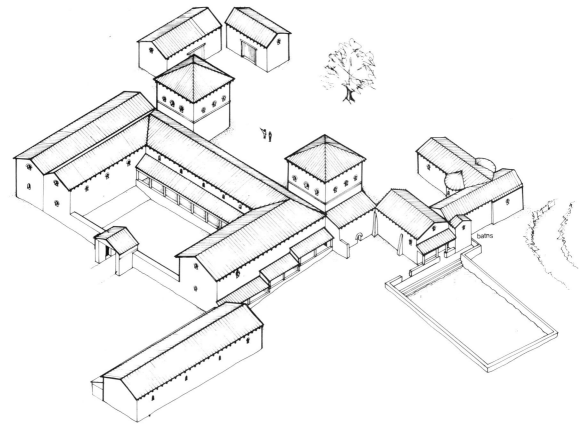

68 *Reconstructed isometric view of the villa at Gadebridge Park (Hertfordshire) as it may have appeared in the early fourth century just prior to its demolition. The main block was built into a slope and contained architectural evidence for the existence of upper storeys. To the east lay the bath suite with its substantial open air pool.* (Based on axonometric reconstructions by David S. Neal but adapted and extended.)

great houses it had its origins in a first-century timber house which grew into a substantial winged-corridor house embellished with towers, outbuildings and a swimming pool (**68**). But by about 360 it had been comprehensively demolished – in archaeological terms in an instant. This seems inexplicable, particularly as agricultural activity continued on the same site in the form of cattle stockades. Such a radical change could be attributed to the political assassination of the owner whose property was seized by the state. There was a possible pogrom following the put-down of the revolt of Magnentius (350-3) who had controlled the

western provinces for instance. But there can never be a certain association in any one case. The estate may simply have been bought by someone else. In contemporary Britain the sheer cost of maintaining expensive houses has proved too onerous for some landowners who move into smaller homes nearby but continue to own and work their estates.

Even houses which remained in use, Lullingstone for instance, show changes in the type of occupation. A mosaic and wall-paintings may have been installed in the late fourth century but the bath-suite and nearby granary were demolished. The house was obviously still in use but it looks less like an independent establishment and even more like an occasional residence or perhaps just an elaborate country dining room with house-church attached. Perhaps it had been incorporated into another estate. At Brixworth, mentioned above (p.66), is a house whose new fourth-century bath-suite was never apparently fired. Perhaps this house too, and its land, was incorporated into a bigger estate. There is no satisfactory resolution to this problem but by the fifth century the economic and social structure which the villas depended on had ceased to exist (see Chapter 8).

The working population of the Romano-British countryside

The very limited material relating to villas and towns allows some image of the people who owned them to be pieced together. It is much harder to build up a similar picture of the rest of the rural population, though the coming of literacy meant that some left records of their names. Some minor town sites have names which indicate that they lay in tracts of land which had originally belonged to an individual. *Sulloniacae*, Brockley Hill, just to the northwest of London, was a small settlement centred on a potting community which specialized in the production of mixing bowls (*mortaria*) and flagons. Its name is thought possibly to derive from a name like Sullonius, perhaps the owner of the land. The names of a number of potters who worked there and in other nearby locations in the late first and early second centuries are known from the stamps on their products, such as Doinus, Marinus and Matugenus. Their names are Celtic types and they would almost certainly have been able to trace their origins amongst the local farming communities.

There are isolated instances of individuals who were in charge of the countryside in an official capacity. At Combe Down near Bath an inscription erected between 212 and 217 recorded the restoration of a headquarters building by an imperial freedman called Naevius. Perhaps the house with which it was associated was actually part of an imperial estate, even though it had been allowed to decay. At Bath an inscription recording repair work in the town was erected by a centurion called Gaius Severius Emeritus who describes himself as 'centurion of the region'.

For the remainder of the rural population it is practically impossible to say anything about the individuals. Villages like Catsgore have produced nothing which would tell us about the kind of people who lived there. They may have been tied to a nearby villa but equally they may not. Tombstones are almost entirely associated with towns and forts, which means that they cannot be used as evidence for the rural population. Graves are not found in sufficient quantity to produce meaningful statistical evidence about life expectancy. Even villa mausolea are exceptional – the Lullingstone mausoleum,

which contained the skeletons of two anonymous young adults, apart from infant burials, housed the only physical remains of all the individuals who lived there over a period of nearly four centuries. At Bancroft (Buckinghamshire) the mausoleum was robbed out while at Keston (Kent) (see **105**) most of the burials were cremations. Only when large numbers of infant burials are found on a single rural site can we suggest the existence of a slave-run establishment and the exposure of unwanted offspring borne by female slaves. Almost a hundred were found in the yard of the villa at Hambleden (Buckinghamshire) for example.

Stronger evidence comes from some of the names asociated with rural industry. Most of these have been found in connection with ceramic products. One of the most flamboyant was Cabriabanus who seems to have worked as a manufacturer of tiles in west Kent during the second century. He favoured the use of an elaborate roller-die bearing his name, which he applied to flue-tiles (**69**). Other flue-tile manufacturers, such as those who worked in the tilery at the Ashtead villa (Surrey), were no less creative, using abstract and naturalistic motifs (see **79**), but unlike Cabriabanus most were content with adding initials or remained anonymous. Rural potters are equally poorly known even though the practice of stamping products was well-established on imported samian ware and Romano-British *mortaria*. An isolated instance from the Oxfordshire area is one Tamesubugus

69 *Tile from Plaxtol (Kent), bearing the impression of a roller-die carrying the name Cabriabanus.*

who scratched his name on to a *mortarium* he had made prior to firing it in the third or fourth century. His name seems to have been derived from where he worked in the upper reaches of the river Thames, *Tamesis*. This makes it almost certain that his family originated in the area and were Celtic even though his name had been 'latinized'.

Sculptors and masons are known mostly from urban and military contexts but a few instances in the countryside have been identified. Firminus had his name carved on a stone at the Barnsley Park villa (Gloucestershire) in the form *Firmini* which means 'of Firminus'. This may either refer to the Villa of Firminus (as with the *Villa Faustini* above) or perhaps *Officina Firmini*, 'the workshop of Firminus', meaning that he was the builder; both are possible, though the latter is more likely given the context of a building stone. A votive relief from Bisley (Gloucestershire) depicts a male military figure with helmet, shield and spear. It almost certainly once stood on display in a rural shrine and bears an inscription recording that it was dedicated to the god Romulus (represented as Mars) by one Gulioepius, a name of Celtic origin, but that it was carved by Iuventinus, a very Roman name. Another relief found nearby has no inscription but is very similar in style and was probably carved by Iuventinus too. Perhaps Iuventinus worked at the shrine, carving reliefs to order and selling them to people who wished to make a dedication. A similar type of dedication was inscribed on the plinth of a small bronze statue of Mars which was then deposited into the Fossdyke at Torksey (Lincolnshire). The inscription records that it was made by Celatus the coppersmith out of bronze at the expense of two brothers, Bruccius and Caratius Colasunius (**70**). However, as with many votive objects the context and the inscription give us no information about where the people lived or where the statue was made.

70 *Bronze figure of Mars from the Fossdyke, Torksey (Lincolnshire). The plinth records the dedicants, the bronzesmith and the cost of its manufacture. Height 27cm (10½in). (British Museum.)*

6

The rural economy

Problems with the Romano-British economy

An economy is the system by which a community generates and distributes its wealth. In order to understand accurately how an economy works a great deal of information is needed. The archaeological record is a poor source of such material because it is made up of information which originated at different times, drawn both randomly and selectively from a number of different places. The best evidence is found in towns where the sheer quantity of material is likely to give the best overall picture but even here the evidence is almost entirely confined to non-perishables such as pottery. The movement of food, fundamental to any economy, is therefore even more difficult to understand and this is of especial importance when considering the countryside.

In order to make some sense out of how the ancient world managed its resources we have to rely to some extent on occasional observations made by contemporary historians or other writers. But for the most part there is no choice but to make the best of the archaeological record. From this we can do no more than build up a general picture and it is very important to stand back from trying to be too specific – the quality of the data is simply not good enough to withstand such scrutiny. It is clear that Roman Britain was fundamentally a rural place – but then so was almost everywhere in the ancient world. That did not change throughout the period of Roman rule though the countryside seems to have become more ordered, perhaps with some significant technical improvements in agricultural techniques. The introduction of a co-ordinated and maintained system of communications will have had

a critical influence in drawing the whole countryside into the economy. The most noticeable change was that Britain became more self-contained and independent, reflected in political events of the latter part of the third century. By looking at aspects of Romano-British history and archaeology it is possible to see something of how the economy functioned, and trace the connections with the pre-Roman period discussed in Chapter 1.

Taxation and tribute

The imperial government was a permanent and pervasive influence in the working of any part of the Roman economy; in a heavily garrisoned and geographically small province like Britain this influence was particularly strong. Britain was an 'expensive' province because it contained a relatively large army. There were never less than three legions, and during the conquest phase there were four (almost a sixth of the legionary total of the Empire). Together with the auxiliary forces the provincial garrison amounted to at least 40,000 men. In addition an unknown number of bureaucrats and other government officials were also being paid by the government.

It is unlikely that the new province was able to supply enough food to support all these people in the early years. The military conquest will have severely disrupted the agricultural cycle and we can be sure that the army will have appropriated any stored food or animal herds that it could locate. Even if the situation had settled down by the 50s Tacitus says that the Boudican Revolt in 60 led to famine because at least two years' worth of harvest was lost in large parts of the south-east. Excavations in London have yielded remains of imported grain from the early period of the town's development and this indicates that the town's hinterland was unable to produce enough food to support an urban population too.

The best clue as to how this affected the countryside comes from Tacitus in his account of Agricola's life. Agricola, governor between 78 and 84, is said to have uncovered racketeering. The native farmers were being obliged to hand over grain in excessive amounts to supply the army, probably as a form of taxation in kind, or as a compulsory purchase. This left them short for their own requirements and they had to buy back some of their own produce, but at inflated prices. Not only that but some were being forced to transport the grain to distant forts. Agricola terminated these abuses, though we can assume that grain was still handed over for the army's use. The general absence of coins on early rural sites, compared to their frequency in towns and forts, coupled with the erratic supply of coinage in the first century is often taken to mean that other taxes were also paid in kind. However, if farmers were obliged to pay in cash too, that money would have to be obtained by selling goods in towns and forts, which is where the taxes would be paid. Coinage is normally lost in places where transactions take place. So towns and forts are exactly where the coins should be, and indeed are, found.

The process may have been more indirect for some farmers. Where land taxation involved the old tribal hierarchy it is quite probable that landowners exacted produce from tenants to sell at a profit to raise tax money. The profit then stayed with the landowners, and this would be another factor in slowing rural development, though facilitating the accumulation of personal wealth for a few. In particular we might consider the client kings known to have existed in early Roman Britain, for example Cogidubnus in the south and Prasutagus in East Anglia. The need to obtain cash to pay taxes usually stimulates markets where the produce can be sold. This may have been partly behind the growth of towns at around this time, where a large, agriculturally unproductive, population existed, even though it is clear that the urban population was partially supplied with food imports.

The effect of all this on the rural population would have been to diminish their 'spare' income at least during the first century, though

if abuses took place there was at least a recourse to official protection. Under the old tribal system they may have had a great deal more taken off them by the élite to use for export to pay for luxury goods. As the infrastructure of the province was developed and the effects of military conquest faded into the past the rural economy in much of the province would have stabilized. The agricultural cycle would have become reasonably settled, stimulated by demand from the army and towns, by the need to pay taxes and the attractions of manufactured goods available in towns, but not exhausted. Many of the goods which were confined to towns in the first century began to find their way into the countryside in the second century and this trend continued.

During the fourth century the position altered in favour of the large landowners once more. Taxes were now levied almost exclusively in kind and the actual amounts had increased. The principal reasons for this were the cost of fighting civil and frontier wars, and the considerable inflation of the period and its effect on coinage. Silver, previously the staple precious metal for payment of taxes or storage of wealth, was issued erratically during the late third and fourth centuries. Diocletian (284–305) reorganized the system so that the Empire's annual requirements were divided up into local obligations based on the rural population and the division of agricultural land into assessable units. Each year the amount of goods due per unit was calculated by the government, and levied by local officials drawn from the town councils; the councils were liable for shortfalls. Not only did these levies include the provision of grain but anything else required to maintain imperial administration and the army. A panegyric to Constantius, written at the end of the third century, stressed the enormous agricultural value of Britain to the Empire and how important it was that the province was not lost.

It has been argued that the need to pay increased taxes stimulated agricultural production, though ironically it has become normal to argue exactly the opposite for our own world. It may be that the wealthier villa owners held sufficiently high status to buy their way out of paying taxes through conveniently directed back-handers, and perhaps they enlarged their estates through buying land from people eager to avoid paying land taxes. The evidence for the collection of taxes in the fourth century is limited and variable, though there is some suggestion that the wealthier members of the community frequently evaded taxation, and in some cases may even have ceased to hold public office on the town councils in order to avoid liability for shortfalls. Villa building tailed off in the second half of the fourth century. This could be attributed either to more effective taxation or, as is more likely, the demand for foodstuffs from the army and towns had declined to such a low level that wealth could no longer be earned from a surplus.

Once substantial landed wealth has been established, continued expansion becomes easier to sustain because of the availability of surplus, assuming that a demand exists to stimulate the production of a surplus. In this way land can be bought, more profits accumulated, more spare money spent on display and so on. At the time property represented the only truly secure investment of capital, and it became even more attractive as the supply of silver and gold coin became erratic.

Villas were certainly not necessarily always (and sometimes never) occupied by their owners – they might have held several and had each one individually managed by a bailiff or tenant while they themselves lived in a town during the winter, moving to one of their villas in the summer.

Tenancy was a customary form of land tenure. The arrangement was normally contingent on the annual renewal of a lease but by the fourth century, tenants had become legally tied to the estates on which they worked. This was to make the collection of tax in kind easier to administer and enforce. Tenancy also helped make up the shortfall in slave labour, the availability of which had become a problem as the Roman Empire ceased to expand by the reign of Hadrian (117–38), and this was aided by making tenancy hereditary in the fourth century. Large landowners therefore leased out larger numbers of small units in their estates to tenants (who were frequently ex-slaves). The increase in tenancy goes some way to explaining the growth in the number of rural sites in the fourth century and it also must have promoted the interests of landowners who no longer had to feed their slaves or provide accommodation. Instead they could exact what they wanted from the tenants, who had no alternative except becoming vagrants. The

whole system, which lasted much longer in Gaul than it did in Britain, is often described as containing the roots of medieval feudal serfdom.

The extraction of natural resources

Mining metals and other natural resources was one of the most obvious means of extracting further wealth from a province (see p.42ff.). Sources of metal were usually held in imperial ownership and managed by imperial officials or the military, one of the best examples being the iron industry of the Weald administered by the fleet. In the case of precious metals, and silver is the most relevant example for Britain, the need for bullion to strike coin would have been of paramount importance and we can probably assume that silver mined by the government was exported from Britain to the mint in Rome. The rebel emperor Carausius struck a limited amount of silver coinage in Britain during his brief reign (286–93) and it was of good quality.

Some surviving lead ingots indicate the existence of private companies engaged in mining. They will have leased a mine from the government in return for half the proceeds. An example from Hexgrave Park (Nottinghamshire) carries an inscription recording the name of one Gaius Julius Protus, and states that the pig is of British origin from the mines at *Lutudarum*, a mining centre which was probably near Matlock (Derbyshire). How metal not intended for the government's use was introduced into the market is unknown. The existence of many small manufacturing concerns in the towns, for example the Verulamium bronze-workers or the Malton goldsmith, and the substantial increase in the production of goods like bronze brooches (imports aside), make it clear that metal was readily available. Being reusable, metal goods are not usually found in great quantities on rural sites (**71**).

Stone was probably cut in quarries under imperial ownership, or which had been leased out by the state. Britain is rich in sources of different types of stone, some of which were being exploited by the 60s to supply London and the successive houses at Fishbourne, though much of the more durable varieties like granite and sandstone are distributed mainly in the north and west. Limestone is more prevalent in the central and southern part of the island, and a number of Roman limestone quarries have been identified in the Mendips.

71 *Bronze flagon from Faversham (Kent). The handle depicts Diana and Actaeon. Height 18cm (7in).* (British Museum.)

In general stone was extracted as close to where it was needed as possible and to a large extent this meant making do with what there was. Owners of villas in the Cotswolds like Chedworth made use of the widely available and easily worked local limestone (**72**). A site like Lullingstone in Kent, remote from any source of stone suitable for dressing, was typical of villas and towns of the area in being built out of ragstone concreted together. Kentish ragstone was even shipped to London for use in building work. A wrecked late second-century

72 *Stone column from the villa at Chedworth (Gloucestershire).*

boat at Blackfriars was found to contain a cargo of ragstone brought from near Maidstone, perhaps for use in a major public building project, like the city walls which were built from this material. Although most of the ornamental stone used in the provincial capital and other towns came from places around the Mediterranean, British marble from Purbeck and Alwalton was also used.

Imperial possessions also extended to 'imperial estates', land which was the personal property of the emperor and which was exploited for his personal benefit. The economic effect on areas held as imperial or private estates would have been to restrict the accumulation of private surplus wealth, and therefore effectively to remove regional groups of the rural population out of the provincial economy. A characteristic of these areas is a lack of villas, though as we have seen this dearth of affluence is as easily attributable to a lack of fertile and easily farmed land. There was a great deal of scattered salt production around the Wash during the Iron Age and the Roman period. If the Fens were part of an imperial estate the presence of salt may have been a factor; certainly the proximity of major drainage works which facilitated the development of large-scale salt production points to official activity. However, there were also other sources in Essex, and close to the legionary fortress at Chester. Salt was an exceptionally important commodity in towns or remote settlements because of its use in the preservation of food, especially when the movement of consumables became more limited during the winter.

There are other areas of Britain which appear to have been surprisingly devoid of villas. A number were scattered in the vicinity of several river valleys which cross Akeman Street in Oxfordshire and Gloucestershire yet only a few miles to the south in the Upper Thames Valley there were virtually none at all. Instead there were numerous basic or native settlements. These may have been occupied by workers on an imperial farming estate. At any one time a villa may have been confiscated for a variety of reasons – in such cases the house and all its land was worked entirely for the emperor's benefit. While we know this to have happened we cannot identify it at any one site, except Combe Down in Avon where an inscription indicates the possibility of official ownership.

The countryside and towns – the economic background

It is impossible to avoid the conclusion that villas and towns were inextricably linked by social and economic ties and were to some extent a product of one another. The towns with the greatest density of villas around them were generally also the largest (with the exception of London). Norton Disney (Lincolnshire) is an example of a roadside villa site which appears to have been the product of its location close to the major town at Lincoln. In Northamptonshire, one example among many other areas, the distribution of villas is biased to locations close to roads or rivers while 'non-villa' settlements tend to proliferate not only in these areas but also the more remote regions in between.

Although it is normally impossible to *demonstrate* that a villa owner made use of a river or road to transport produce, the circumstances of many sites make this likely. Several villas in the valley of the Darenth (Kent), including Lullingstone, lie very close to the river. At Eccles on the Medway not far to the east, possible evidence of a landing for boats was found close to the villa. At Alan's Farm, Plaxtol, also in Kent, a conspicuous marshy area at the bottom of the slope directly below the villa on the banks of the river Bourne may be the remains of a small sheltered mooring now silted up. In the north and west where there were few towns there was little or no economic stimulation of the type which would have encouraged the growth of villas, there are consequently very few villas except in a few areas like the Vale of York.

The villa-town relationship was almost certainly more or less suspended during the winter. Laurie Lee's celebrated account of his childhood in a remote Cotswold village during the 1910s is probably not so very far removed from aspects of rural life in Roman Britain. In *Cider with Rosie* he describes winter as a time of routine rural self-sufficiency with roads cut off and streams frozen over. At the beginning of the eighteenth century the elderly diarist and landowner John Evelyn wrote out advice for his grandson and heir in managing the family estate at Wotton in Surrey. In the document *Memoires for my Grand-Son* he recommended that in the winter 'your boat be lock'd and chain'd up' clearly indicating that it would not normally be used at that time of year.

73 *Bronze wheel hub, probably from a cart, found by the the villa at Lullingstone (Kent). Diameter 6.3cm (2½in).* (English Heritage.)

Unfortunately it is very much harder to understand what form the economic relationship took, though it is reasonable to assume that places closer to communications were more likely to benefit from an economic relationship with towns and therefore turn into villas. The role of towns as markets seems only natural and all towns of regional significance had forums – an open market place sited in the town centre. Towns were undoubtedly as much a part of official development as the introduction of an army, the building of roads or mining projects. They had an important social and political role to play by acting as regional centres of influence and control.

Towns also acted as significant concentrations of population and this, as far as the countryside was concerned, meant a major source of demand and therefore stimulation for the agricultural economy. The clustering of villas around the road networks makes it likely that produce was transported to towns along them. The Verulamium (north-east) gate at Cirencester was a relatively elaborate structure with four passageways, two for foot traffic and a central pair for two-way wheeled traffic – the road metalling was worn with wheel ruts from carts and other horse-drawn vehicles moving in and out of the town, many probably carrying agricultural produce. Local economies

were not necessarily purely parochial and we should not underestimate the ability of the Romano-British to move goods. As noted above (p.49), in the eighteenth century cattle were being driven right across the country on time-honoured and traditional routes.

The only surviving evidence for wheeled transport from villas comes in the form of occasional finds of wheel hubs (**73**) and iron linch-pins used to secure wheels to axles. There is no surviving evidence of any one journey which would give us an idea of the speed of travel in Roman Britain. However, Samuel Pepys, the diarist, recorded on 15 July 1661 that he rode from London to Cambridge in the space of four hours, leaving at three o'clock in the morning and arriving at seven. He had time to visit a barber before surprising his brother in bed at eight. The distance covered was approximately 80km (50 miles) on a road probably in a much worse state of repair than it had been in antiquity. This single instance shows that it can be very easy to overestimate the impact of motorized transport and roads, especially where comparatively restricted distances of a few dozen miles are concerned. A villa owner with reasonable access to a major road could clearly expect to be able to travel to a larger market town at least 80km (50 miles) away, carry out his business and return in a day or two. The more widely distributed small towns would have been even easier to reach and would have served most day-to-day requirements. Freight would obviously take longer, but 10 or 15 miles in a day was probably realistic under good conditions. The Welsh drovers of more modern times were accustomed to journeys lasting several weeks.

The bulk of the population would have been involved in farming in some shape or form as appropriate to local conditions and demand. The area around Frilford in Oxfordshire (a temple and market site) has several villas in close proximity to a number of rural farmsteads and native settlements. Some of these may have operated together as parts of the same economic unit, particularly those contained in a single area defined by roads and rivers. In Cirencester a pair of late fourth-century houses within the town walls seem to have been built as farms; if the interpretation of function is correct we do not know if the owners farmed land outside the fortifications. As a general observation villas are normally few and far between in the immediate vicinity of a town, suggesting that some of this land was farmed by town dwellers.

The relationship between villas and towns becomes more complicated when considering the fourth century. It has been argued that urban populations declined at this time, a theory based largely on density of known housing. However, this makes the large numbers of extensive fourth-century urban cemeteries difficult to explain, and denies the villas, whose development is beyond question, the substantial markets surely fundamental to growing rural wealth; though these markets were not necessarily exclusively domestic. In pre-Roman Britain agricultural produce was traded for luxury goods imported from the Continent. Naturally there is no archaeological evidence for the exports while the imports of silver, glass and pottery are generally found in wealthy aristocratic graves.

Perhaps in fourth-century Britain the same pattern had recurred due to the unpredictable state of the frontier in north-east Gaul and Germany, only this time the agricultural produce was shipped out via the towns with payment to the villa owners either coming in the form of gold and silver coin or as luxury goods such as silver plate. There is a quite significant increase in the appearance of such goods at this time in Britain, though in a variety of contexts. They include the Water Newton Christian treasure, the Mildenhall hoard of plate (see **43**) and the Thetford treasure made up largely of jewellery (**colour plate 15**) and silver spoons (see **96**). None can be directly associated with villas but all were made up of objects of very high value. They certainly fit the context of an upper tier of society well able to afford expensive mosaics and substantial structural extensions to their rural homes. However, such a theory is purely speculative and there is also the possibility that corrupt tax collecting and the growth of enforced tenancy favoured the wealthy few (see p.86).

Agriculture

It is very rare to find direct evidence of crops except when burnt grain is occasionally found in corn-drying ovens, as at Barton Court Farm, pits, or destroyed buildings. Instead evidence is more usually in the form of pollen or impressions left by grain in tiles or pottery placed on the ground to dry. In addition to Caesar's and

74 *Bronze model of a ploughman and team of ox and cow from the fort at Piercebridge (Durham). Length 5.5cm (2in).* (British Museum.)

75 *Bronze model plough, originally from a group of miniature tools found together at an unknown site, perhaps a grave, in Sussex. Length 9.5cm (4in).* (British Museum.)

Strabo's observations we have writing tablets from the fort at Vindolanda which occasionally mention grain and other food, including barley, wheat, pork and venison, as well as fish sauce, wine and spices which would have been imported from the Continent.

Contemporary ploughs were made almost entirely out of wood and naturally these are virtually unknown, except from statue groups such as the Piercebridge plough team (**74**) or models (**75**). However, the plough share was normally made out of iron, or had an iron tip. These occasionally survive, though during normal use they would gradually have worn out and been melted down to help make another. Improved varieties of ploughs, introduced in the third and fourth centuries, which cut and turned deeper soils, will have made it easier to exploit more land for arable use. Field systems were almost certainly far more widespread than will ever be known. Recent work in Yorkshire and Nottinghamshire has identified extensive traces of land management. Fields were made by dividing up the land into long strips somewhere between 50 and 100m (164 and 328ft) wide. The strips were then subdivided into units averaging about 1.5 ha (4 acres). Such land division may have been organized early in the Roman period, though so far excavations point to a date in the third and fourth centuries.

Farming and agricultural techniques would have been based on traditional methods as well as innovations and technical improvements imported from the Continent. The latter were by no means necessarily the consequence of the invasion. Indeed one study has shown that improvements such as rotary querns appeared in the early part of the first millennium BC while even systematic drainage was being organized in the first century BC. The evidence suggests the use of prehistoric field systems reached its height in the second half of the first millennium BC. Most of the improvements which occurred in the first century AD, becoming widespread in the third and fourth centuries, are 'architectural' or technical, such as large granaries on villa estates (for example Lullingstone), water-powered mills or corn-drying ovens. These, and improved tools, point to a degree of processing taking place in the countryside in order to supply a more finished product, and in bulk, something which must reflect the nature of Romano-British demand. Even crop rotation may have been practised. At this distance it is extremely difficult to be certain how farming was actually carried out in any one case.

Other evidence for the processing of the grain comes in the form of quernstones (**76**), found on almost all types of occupation sites. Some were made of imported volcanic lava but a quarry for quartz sandstone querns has been located at Lodsworth (West Sussex). Querns from the quarry seem to have been used in a number of places across central southern Britain. The quarry was in operation in the late Iron Age, with maximum production taking place during the first century AD, reflecting the development of agriculture before the Roman conquest. Another quern factory exploiting similar stone may have existed for a similar timespan at or near a slightly later villa site on

76 *Rotary quern (lower part) found at Ham, near Poole (Dorset), but made of stone from Niedermendig in Germany. Diameter 61cm (24in).* (British Museum.)

the coast near Folkestone (Kent). The villa was excavated in the 1920s before it started collapsing over the cliff edge. The querns, which include a number of unfinished examples, have been recovered in recent years from the foreshore. They seem to have been distributed over a wide area in Kent. Querns range in size from hand-operated types to the more substantial examples used in water-powered mills such as those known at various locations near Hadrian's Wall.

Grain could be stored in barns, and examples have been identified at a number of villa sites. The Lullingstone villa had a barn, while in its earliest phase a room with a sunken floor and ramp may have been used to store grain. The Littlecote hall and baths complex seems to have been built out of the adapted remains of a barn. The so-called 'corn-driers' (**77**) are a common feature of late rural sites, for example at Stanwick, Barton Court Farm and Brading. They resemble kilns in having furnaces with a flue which carried hot air to an upper chamber where corn may have been dried; some, however, are thought more likely to have been used for warming and drying barley as part of the fermentation process to make malt for beer. As an interesting aside a writing tablet from the fort at Vindolanda (dated around the beginning of the second century) records various foodstuffs used at the fort and this includes *cervesa* (or *cervesia*) which means 'Celtic beer' – no doubt a Romano-British product.

In the discussion about villa layouts in the

77 *Stone corn-drier from the villa at Stanwick (Northamptonshire), during the site's excavation.* (English Heritage.)

previous chapter the possibility that some out-buildings were used to house animals was suggested. These buildings are normally quite simple but have floor drainage gullies to aid clearance of natural waste products. Even some of the buildings at a modest village like Cats-

gore had such facilities (**78**). Better evidence for pastoral farming comes in the form of animal bones. The Gadebridge Park villa, for example, produced a large number of bone fragments indicating the presence of cattle and sheep, as well as a smaller proportion of pigs. However, with the absence of any reliable means of preserving meat for long periods, animals must have been kept alive for as long as possible. The only method of preserving meat was salting it,

93

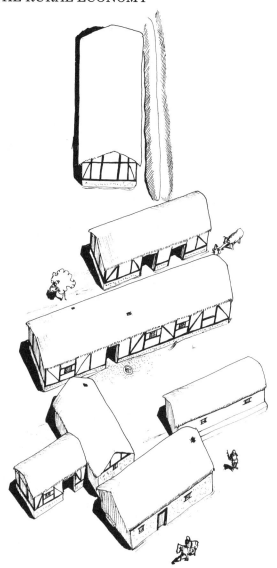

78 *Reconstructed axonometric view of one of the farmsteads which which made up the village settlement at Catsgore (Somerset), as it may have appeared some time between the late second and mid-fourth centuries.*

hence the importance of the salt industry in Roman Britain. Animals intended for sale as meat would have been walked to markets in towns or villages, over distances which could have been very considerable. This is still normal practice in many countries today.

Animal bones are also found on temple sites, almost certainly as a result of sacrifice. They may have been brought as individual offerings by pilgrims, or reared at the site for sale. In such cases the animals found tend to reflect those associated with the local deity. For Roman Britain a study of animal bones from different kinds of sites has shown an interesting trend from the most romanized to the least romanized. At the latter, sheep tend to predominate, perhaps in part reflecting their tolerance of more marginal land, with a small proportion of cattle. For military and major urban sites the picture is reversed with oxen accounting for up to 70 per cent of the bones, and pigs making up a further 20. This could be partly attributable to better land but it is also likely that as cattle command higher prices, with more and better quality meat 'per pound', they were far more likely to be, and capable of being, moved from remoter areas to be sold in towns and forts where demand for such meat was highest (see p.49). In other words the evidence for the butchery and consumption of meat is not necessarily evidence for the distribution of pastoral farming. At some long-term villa sites, such as Frocester Court (Gloucestershire), the animal pattern altered during the Roman period with an increase in ox bones from about a quarter to nearly two-thirds of period assemblages at the expense, mainly, of sheep. This probably reflects an adaptation to demand.

Timber

Timber is a primary natural resource. It is easy to forget its limitless applications and the need for the careful management of woodlands. Caesar observed that timber of all types could be obtained in Britain, except beech and fir. Hiding in woodlands allowed Cassivellaunus to evade Caesar's army in 54 BC. Unfortunately the literary sources for Roman Britain do not tell us much more. Instead an interesting glimpse of the kind of problems which may have faced those concerned with the exploitation of Roman Britain's forests comes from much later. In 1662 John Evelyn was asked by the Royal Society to write a book about the problems resulting from excessive forest clearance during the English Civil War. In *Sylva* (1664) Evelyn, who was an expert on trees, wrote, 'it has not been the increase of shipping alone, the multiplication of Glass-works, Iron-Furnaces, and the like, from whence this impolitick diminution of our Timber has proceeded; but from the disproportionate spreading of Tillage'. He described the result as

94

'devastation' and proceeded to set down as much practical advice as he could glean from his own experience and also from foresters and woodmen on his family's, and other estates.

Evelyn indicates exactly the causes of depletion which would have been relevant to Roman Britain also: military and industrial demand for wood as building material and fuel, and the clearance of forest for agriculture – it has already been shown that there is a great deal of evidence for a considerable increase in agriculture both before and during the Roman period. To these we can add the domestic and commercial demands of towns. It has been computed that the legionary fortress at Caerleon would have required 150ha (380 acres) of woodland to build. Thereafter maintenance would have required more. To begin with wood would have been cut as and where needed by the military. There would have been no opportunity to establish stocks of seasoned wood. As demand from the towns grew and the wood first used began to rot, so it would have become essential to establish stocks. Of course clearance for agriculture would have provided a supply but as can be seen in modern times, clearance has nothing to do with demand for, or easy access to, wood and waste can be colossal.

It is not evident that woodland was systematically managed in Roman Britain. In London wooden piles destroyed in a Hadrianic (117–38) fire had come from trees only cut down in c.100. Analysis of tree-ring dates from timbers used in the New Fresh Wharf in London has indicated that the early third century quay was built principally from mature oak trees cut down at around that time. By as soon as the mid-third century these resources had already diminished to the extent that younger trees were being used. The iron-working site at Beauport Park (Sussex) fell out of use at around this time for unknown reasons. Administered by the fleet, the woods in the area would have been exploited for charcoal for smelting fuel, and possibly also for ship-building. It is likely that over-exploitation of timber had made it impossible to continue either activity. As the Roman period lasted slightly less than four centuries it is just possible that a decline in timber stocks did not have a truly critical effect but it does seem likely that timber was taken for granted and little care was taken to preserve it. Of course the principal damage would have been done in the first and second centuries, when the

occupants of forts and towns would have been responsible for clearing large areas in their hinterlands. The consequences would have lasted for many generations as we know to our own cost.

Rural industries
Evidence for rural industries is widespread, in particular for the building industry. The owners of the Ashtead villa (Surrey) operated a tile kiln for the manufacture of unusually elaborately decorated flue-tiles (**79a**). Some were transported for use in the villa at Beddington 13.5km (9 miles) away, unless they were manufactured on the spot by tile-makers sent there for the purpose. Another rural tile kiln has been located at Hartfield (East Sussex). Established around the beginning of the second century the kiln may have been built to produce tiles for an unlocated villa, or for buildings associated with a nearby ironworks.

The Hartfield kiln (Sussex) contained a number of unused roof tiles when found. It had been used to produce an extensive variety of tiles, including some impressed with a patterned roller-die. The die used has been recognized elsewhere (for example Colchester and Verulamium), so it is likely that the kiln was built and operated by tilers who moved around from place to place looking for work, something which the flamboyant Cabriabanus (see **69**) may also have done (see p.83). The designs used are interesting not just because of their archaeological value in showing clear patterns of distribution, but also because their practical purpose was to provide a surface which would help key cement: the patterns were invisible in use. They may have played a role in marketing – we might call it a 'product image'. At the very least they suggest a degree of sophistication amongst rural industries. Other markings are common on tiles, for example signatures (**79b**) or records of tile batches (**79c**). Such marks were probably made on site when a tiler was producing tiles close to where they were needed.

Tiles are heavy and fragile so it is unlikely that many were moved any great distance from their place of manufacture, though the stamped products of a tile-kiln at Minety (Wiltshire), mainly active up to the middle of the third century, were used quite widely in the cantonal area of the Dobunni (governed from Cirencester). Tile-makers were probably typical of

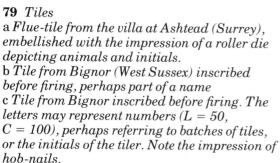

79 *Tiles*
*a Flue-tile from the villa at Ashtead (Surrey),
embellished with the impression of a roller die
depicting animals and initials.*
*b Tile from Bignor (West Sussex) inscribed
before firing, perhaps part of a name*
*c Tile from Bignor inscribed before firing. The
letters may represent numbers (L = 50,
C = 100), perhaps referring to batches of tiles,
or the initials of the tiler. Note the impression of
hob-nails.*

other types of itinerant rural craftsmen who
made a living touring their region seeking
building or farming work – though unlike the
tile-makers we cannot discern their work so
easily, unless they were mosaicists. Itinerant
craftsmen are by their very nature difficult to
trace. One exceptionally rare instance is the
hoard buried by a metalworker at Snettisham
in Norfolk (**80**). The contents of the hoard seem
to be the work and stock-in-hand of someone
engaged in the manufacture of jewellery. He
had over one hundred unmounted gemstones
and a quantity of scrap metal and coins. The
coins and scrap were probably for melting
down, particularly interesting because the
bronze coins belong to the late second century

while the silver examples were nearly a hundred years older or more. They were made of
silver purer than that available in the late
second century and this was doubtless why the
hoarder had chosen them.

In the first and second centuries evidence for
other rural industries is fairly limited. Metals
were being extracted but they were either
shipped abroad, or used by the army or urban
artisans. Metalworking must have existed in
the countryside but it did not have a particularly high profile. Pottery was being manufactured in most settlements at some time or
another but most Romano-British pottery
industries of consequence at that date were
associated with the towns. Rural pottery industries were probably seasonal and distributed
their products very locally. The potters
belonged to a tradition of manufacturing serviceable vessels, suitable for cooking and storage, that were also cheap, especially when
hand-made and fired in bonfires known as
'clamps'. There were some major rural pottery
industries, for example in the Severn Valley,
and the more important kitchen-ware industries scattered around the Thames Estuary and
in Dorset (Poole) (**81**). Known as the Black-
Burnished pottery industries the latter pair

80 *Jeweller's hoard from Snettisham (Norfolk), together with the pot in which the material was found.* (British Museum.)

produced a range of simple utilitarian dishes and pots in a well-established style. They were bought in enormous quantities by the Roman army during the second century and later.

The Dorset products (now called 'Black-Burnished 1') were handmade but were widely distributed in the western part of Britain with concentrations on the military sites of the northern frontier up until the fourth century

81 *Black-Burnished pottery (about ¼ scale).* a *and* b *are typical of the second-century products of the Dorset handmade BB1 varieties.* d *is a comparable product of the Thames Estuary BB2 wheel-thrown industry,* c *is a later BB2 product, probably fourth century.*

when the market collapsed to a much more localized level in the south-west. For the Thames Estuary products (known as 'Black-Burnished 2'), distribution was more polarized with distinct areas of distribution in Kent and East Anglia and on the northern frontier, despite having the added sophistication of being wheelmade. It was also only distributed in this way during the second century. The potters worked in isolated places around the coast, for example at Cooling or Higham on the north Kent marshes, and it is quite possible that production was seasonal, perhaps as an additional income-earner to farming. If the army was buying produce for shipment to the north then this would explain why it was possible to ship such low value pottery all the way to Scotland, which otherwise makes little sense.

The fine-ware market, up until the end of the second century, was catered for either by the

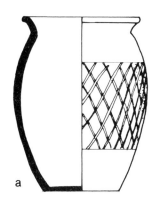

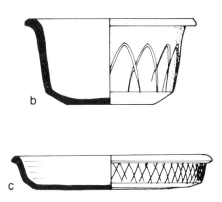

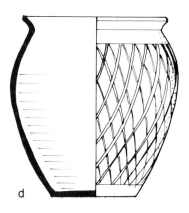

urban industries, for example at Colchester, or by imports, the most important of which was Gaulish samian found on almost every site of the first and second centuries (82). The reason for the collapse of the samian industry is unknown, but collapse it did and by the early years of the third century it had ceased to have any significance at all in Roman Britain. Its place was filled in part by rural Romano-British pottery industries which had already been in existence for some time but on a very limited scale.

In general, pottery at this period was no longer moved over enormous distances – the distribution patterns of the new industries were much more restricted than those of the former giant fine-ware producers on the Continent, though they were much greater than Romano-British industries had previously enjoyed. Chief amongst these new pottery industries were the scattered kiln sites of the Oxfordshire region. Lying in the upper reaches of the Thames and its tributaries in the heart of Britain, the potters had easy access to the most densely populated part of the province.

By the middle of the third century traditional production of kitchen wares had been broadened into a much wider range. Kitchen wares were still produced but specialist potters manufactured *mortaria* and decorated fine wares. The latter were produced either in red colour-coat with painted decoration or in a white 'parchment' ware with painted decoration. Although the samian mould-decorated technique was not employed, many vessels emulated samian forms which implies that the collapse of the samian industry had nothing to do with the collapse of demand. The scale of production of any individual production site is very difficult to assess but some indication of the intensity of output was found at a recent discovery near Didcot. Here a potter's workshop was excavated along with a waster dump, over 100m (328ft) long and 1.5m (5ft) deep, of pots which had been damaged in the kiln. The site was in operation between the second and fourth centuries but the full extent of pottery manufacture has yet to be discovered.

The new products are found both in towns and on rural sites, especially in the south. Even if the kilns were more widely dispersed the pots themselves were evidently distributed efficiently. The Oxfordshire industry's output was probably only exceeded by the industry of the

82 *Samian bowl (form 37) from the villa at Sedgebrook, Plaxtol (Kent). Found shattered beneath a roof which collapsed when part of the house burnt down in the late second, early third century. Made by Cinnamus of Lezoux, Central Gaul some time in the mid-second century. (See also* **20**.*)*

Nene Valley near the town of Water Newton (Cambridgeshire). Other rural pottery industries were on a smaller scale. The New Forest industry produced vessels which were very similar to those of the Oxfordshire region, but in much smaller numbers. Comparatively rare outside the central southern part of Britain, New Forest wares never made a serious impact on the provincial market.

Interestingly the Oxfordshire wares are common in the New Forest area of distribution, but not vice-versa, which suggests that the New Forest industry (83) was unable even to supply local demand. If so, it was probably a seasonal industry practised by potters who were mainly engaged in agriculture. A northern industry existed at Crambeck near Malton which came to dominate the fine-ware market in the north during the latter part of the fourth century, at the same time as its kitchen products replaced the black-burnished vessels from Dorset. There are several other rural fine-ware industries known, for example at Brampton (Norfolk) or Much Hadham (Hertfordshire) but they operated on a smaller scale.

Kitchen or 'coarse' wares remained predominantly the result of local production. Most rural sites produce a fair quantity of sherds which cannot be identified on more than a handful of other sites in the immediate vicinity. Even so the Lullingstone villa has been shown

83 *Indented beaker made by the third–fourth century pottery industry in the New Forest.* (British Museum.)

pottery industry was established in the first century to exploit the clay, water and fuel – all essential ingredients for a pottery industry. Nearby heathland supplied sand which was needed to temper the clay. This was of particular importance for kitchen wares because the sand helped thicken the clay and restricted the shrinkage which would otherwise occur during firing.

Alice Holt products were widely distributed in central southern England during the first and second centuries. But it was not until after about 270 that they actually came to dominate the coarse-ware market throughout the southeast. The quality of the ware was originally very variable but by the mid-third century firing techniques had been refined, and thereafter most products appear in the same fabric, though the neutral slip could be made to fire either grey or white. The better quality material bears comparison with fine wares and this may have contributed to the industry's success.

It is possible, however, that the industry's growth was incidental to another – it may be that other local produce was being transported out of the area to markets in Alice Holt jars and bowls. Some of the larger narrow-necked jars would have been particularly suitable for the storage of goods like wine and honey. A graffito on an Alice Holt storage jar found at Winchester seems to record its capacity as 8 *urnae* (about 108 litres or 23 gallons), a measurement of liquid. It is therefore a possibility that the Alice Holt potteries were associated with the production of, say, wine, and that this was the real reason for their penetration of the southeast; like the black-burnished pottery it is otherwise difficult to explain how such a basic type of pottery could be worth moving around very far. However, Alice Holt's comparatively late development has been linked to a theoretical increase in taxation in the urban areas, thereby stimulating rural industries to fill the gap. This is, however, only a theory.

Although these pottery industries were only one facet of the Romano-British countryside they provide a useful foundation for archaeologists. The distribution of their products gives an idea of the extent to which rural produce could be moved around the province. New Forest pottery, for example, has a distribution pattern which reflects identifiable communication routes such as roads. In other words where a road was available then the pottery is found

to have had access to about eighty different sources of kitchen wares, some of which came from the Dorset Black-Burnished industry. A group of vessels from Stonea gives an idea of the range of types found on rural sites (**84**). During the third and fourth centuries, however, one rural kitchen-ware industry expanded its production out of all proportion to most others.

This industry was sited in the Alice Holt Forest (Surrey). The land in the area is poorly drained and of little use to agriculture which explains why it is still largely wooded today. A

84 *Group of second-century pottery from the Fenland site at Stonea (Cambridgeshire), including grey kitchen wares, decorated hunt cups (right) and a samian bowl. (front, centre)* (British Museum.)

further from its source than in directions where no road was available. It may well be that the parties responsible for buying up the pottery and distributing it were the same as those who purchased food. As the pottery distribution reflects the importance of the towns in the marketing structure this is another instance where it might be argued that the theory that towns were in significant decline is in error.

Pottery also demonstrates that the rural economy was sufficiently well-organized to enable pottery manufactured in the Oxfordshire area or Alice Holt, for example, to be transported considerable distances. Oxfordshire products in particular achieved a wide penetration right across central, southern and eastern England, and examples have been found as far away as Cornwall, north Wales and on Hadrian's Wall. This growth of rural industries was a characteristic of the third and fourth centuries in Britain and may have been linked to restrictive practices and local taxes in towns. If pottery could be successfully moved in this way then we can assume that food was too. Analysis of the large amount of pottery from Lullingstone showed that in addition to an extensive range of Romano-British wares, pottery, and therefore probably food, had also originated in Gaul, Germany and Spain.

The clear implication from this chapter is that economically successful places produced enough surplus money to pay for villas – this was clearly what a successful landowner generally aspired to having; though we should not ignore the fact that there may have been peoples and areas where wealth was invested in more portable precious metal goods, ones which tend not to be found in the archaeological record. Places where villas are not found must have suffered from distinct disadvantages. These may have been official, in the form of imperial estates, or as part of substantial private estates, but it may also be that there were fundamental economic disadvantages. The absence of urban development is likely to have been central to this: the demand did not exist. The more remote a farmstead was from a town, or even a large village, the less likely it was that its produce could be sold profitably to a non-productive (in agricultural terms) market. Where the quality of the land is simply less good and is subjected to greater extremes of weather, food becomes more difficult to produce; in remote areas the costs of transportation increase. In other words food becomes expensive, and more importantly, it becomes more expensive than that produced in places which enjoyed better soils, better weather and better communications.

The northern and western parts of Roman Britain are largely distinguished by a lack of evidence for participation in the developed rural economy. Not only do villas barely exist but small towns and villages are also virtually non-existent. Imported goods are much rarer.

In the north and in Wales the fort *vici* went some way to fill the gap but in the south-west peninsula forts were almost totally absent. By being more remote from continental influences and occupying marginal land these places were unable to develop the kind of economic surplus which would have allowed them to participate more fully in trade. Sites like Chysauster in Cornwall probably functioned as mainly self-sufficient economic units with only very occasional commercial contact with the outside world. The individuals who lived there are unlikely to have been particularly concerned about this – at such a practical distance from the 'advanced' part of the province the towns and villas were probably viewed with a mixture of mythical fears, ignorance, awe and indifference. Fear of the unknown and of change are common characteristics of remote rural places. Coupled with the essential day-to-day routines of making a living there would have been little time, incentive or opportunity to increase wealth.

7

Rural shrines and temples

The visible face of religion in Roman Britain was classical in character, or at least in intent, but its spirit was Celtic. Nowhere was this as clear as it was in the countryside. In the towns religion was often associated with political interests; for example dedications of allegiance to the spirit of the emperors. Some towns had classical temples, Colchester being the prime example, and these would have served as the focus of such cults. In those temples and their precincts official events in the classical religious calendar would have been celebrated. But these occasions would have been of little concern to the general population who instead favoured the more intimate contact available from less sophisticated and more traditional cults.

Celtic religion was rural and tribal in character because it was closely associated with fertility, virility, strength and the natural cycle of birth and death. Of course this was also nominally true of much classical religion and this made it possible to combine (or 'syncretize') gods who shared characteristics (also called 'attributes'). But whereas urban cults were usually built on virgin sites within the towns, rural cults often seem to have been continued in places which had been sacred long before the coming of the Romans. Very occasionally these cults proved so popular that they developed into towns during the Roman period; Bath is the principal example.

Rural shrines, reliefs and altars were scattered around the province, for example a stone relief from Knights Langley (85). Excavation shows that a temple of Roman date had frequently been placed where offerings had already been made for centuries. The focus of the pre-Roman cult was often no more than a river, a tree, a hill or a spring. One Celtic goddess known from an inscription found at Ilkley was called Verbeia, a name thought to mean 'winding river'. Why any particular spot should have been chosen is generally unknown. Only in a place like Bath, with its hot springs, is the reason self-evident.

Before the Roman Conquest, Celtic gods were rarely portrayed in human form although they were believed to have powers which mirrored human activities, like the warrior hunting gods such as Cocidius. During the Roman period this changed and instead of being shadowy figures lost in the light and shadows of forests, deities were frequently depicted in the form of statues or reliefs. Generally when this occurred the Celtic god had been associated with a classical equivalent, and this supplied a convenient basis for representation, though it was not necessarily a straightforward process. Cocidius, a Celtic warrior god, was matched with Mars in a number of places and in effect the two gods were interpreted as being the same in a combined manifestation. However, at Uley (Gloucestershire), where parts of the cult statue of Mercury have been found (see **110**) some offerings suggest that Mars may also have been used to express some of the attributes of the unknown Celtic god worshipped there before the Roman period. Celtic gods often belonged to very localized areas – the various warrior gods are good examples, but Mars could be combined with many of them.

This process of syncretization had the practical advantage of making it easier to present Roman culture as a benign influence instead of being repressive. It also made it easier to create a stronger sense of social cohesiveness by helping to promote an impression of a provincial

86 *Bronze plaque from the temple at Nettleton (Wiltshire), depicting Apollo and recording that it was a gift of one Decimius. Late third, early fourth century, height 10.7cm (4in).* (After Wedlake.)

85 *Altar from Knights Langley (Gloucestershire), depicting Mars.* (British Museum.)

rather than a tribal culture, particularly important in the countryside where the impact of classical culture and urbanization was less potent. Language played a part in this; the absence of Celtic in a written form meant that Latin (which seems to have become widespread fairly quickly) was automatically associated with worship in a romanized manner, for example on altars or in dedications.

The use of sculpture and written messages to the gods presents us with a more coherent body of evidence for how Romano-Celtic religion was followed. At the heart of much ancient religion was the belief in, and the law of, a contract. Men and women had business-like relationships with the gods which began with a service needed. The deity was approached and the service requested, in return for which the person would make a sacrifice, erect an altar or make some other gift. Records of these requests are very rarely found and instead all that remain are altars or small metal plaques which simply state that the dedicant had fulfilled his vow to the god (**86**), believing that what he or she had asked of the god had been done.

This non-specific and stock formula was used because the nature of the contract remained a confidential arrangement. At a few places, though, the original requests have survived because the people who wrote them did not expect anyone ever to see them. The temple to Mercury at Uley has yielded a large number of 'curses' inscribed on lead tablets. One was written by a man called Cenacus who complained that a father and son called Vitalinus and Natalinus had stolen a draught animal of his. He requested that Mercury ensure that the thieves suffer ill-health until they returned the animal and made an offering to the god. On another a woman called Saturnina called to Mercury for help to secure the return of a stolen piece of linen, a third part of which was promised to the god if it was recovered (**87**). Such requests create an impression of a fairly unsophisticated form of religion, for example concerns about thefts of specific objects are common on these lead tablets.

The tablets frequently refer to offerings, remains of which are among the most common finds on religious sites. They include coins and pieces of jewellery, the latter frequently deliberately damaged perhaps in order to end their connection with the owner. Animal bones can sometimes be used to support the identification of the god worshipped at a particular site. Uley produced large numbers of bones from goats and cockerels, animals known to have been Mercury's 'familiars', and which are often depicted with him in statue groups. The animals were probably sold on the site to visitors and were killed for sacrifice. Of course this kind of relationship with a god is just as easily interpreted as superstition. To what extent devotion existed as a truly deep belief and faith we cannot know. The country shrines were almost certainly just as important as places in which to seek leisure and recreation. Many temples were built in charming locations within reasonable access to communication routes.

Rural cult centres

There were many different types of rural shrines. Some were elaborate complexes of buildings, amounting to small villages. Sited on major roads they were just as likely to have served as thriving centres of local trade and as recreational retreats. The site at Nettleton (Wiltshire) is one of the best examples of this (**88**). The site at Gosbecks Farm near Colchester included a theatre but this religious zone

87 *One of more than 160 lead* defixiones, *'curse' tablets, found on the temple site at Uley (Gloucestershire). This tablet was headed a* commonitorium *(first line – which means literally a note or letter with important information) to Mercury (beginning of second line, curiously erasing the name of Mars-Silvanus which was originally written there) by a woman called Saturnina whose name starts at the end of the second line and carries on to the third. She wished Mercury to help recover a piece of stolen linen cloth and promised one-third of it to him and a third to Silvanus, for assistance. The text carries on to the other side. Actual size 8.3 by 6cm (3 by 2in). (British Museum.)*

was originally a major component of the Iron Age *oppidum* of *Camulodunum* and subsequently remained a peripheral feature of the *colonia* a few miles to the north.

Other shrines were located in places of more practical significance. The temple at Woodeaton (Oxfordshire), for example, lay close to a road junction at Alchester on a line marking the tribal boundary between the Dobunni and the Catuvellauni. This neutral but convenient location may have been behind its probable role as a market or fairground. The nearby temple site at Frilford (Oxfordshire) also lay beside a road and had an amphitheatre of sorts which was probably used for displays and re-enactments of myths on religious festival days. There were single villas close to both Woodeaton and Frilford; perhaps the temples were built by the villa owners in the interests of marketing their own estate produce, as well as for the pleasures of social gatherings at religious events. We cannot know if this was the case

88 *Reconstructed isometric view of the octagonal temple of Apollo at Nettleton (Wiltshire), as it may have appeared c.300–30 prior to the building's partial collapse. (See also* **colour plate 14**.)

or what role the villa owners might have played, but examples from more modern times may give an idea of rural religious traditions and the relationship between religion and landowners. In *Cider with Rosie*, an autobiography of a rural childhood around the time of the First World War, Laurie Lee described the 'Parochial Church Tea and Annual Entertainment' as a midwinter 'orgy of communal gluttony' which masqueraded as a semi-religious gathering. It was introduced by the squire – the local landowner and benefactor of the event. He and the church were regarded as the pivotal features of the annual cycle of festivals. The rural temples and villa owners of Roman Britain may have played host to different occasions, but these traditional activities, now dwindling in the late twentieth century, are useful reminders of the blurring of religious, social and economic

interests which takes place in all real communities to some extent, and particularly so in the countryside.

In addition to these prominent rural temple sites there were also small temples which seem to have stood in virtual isolation, apart from one or two outbuildings. The temple on the former Iron Age hillfort of Maiden Castle (Dorset) is one such case (**89, colour plate 13**). Finally there were isolated shrines which were little more than altars in small stone repositories like the pair on Scargill Moor above Bowes (Durham) or a simple carved relief on a remote hillside like 'Rob of Risingham' near the fort of the same name (see **10**) in Northumberland.

Almost all of these places would have had some sort of cult significance in pre-Roman Britain, but very few Roman temple sites have produced structural evidence for pre-Roman temples. This is almost certainly because the Roman buildings were invariably built in stone at some time in their histories and this naturally tended to obliterate any traces of earlier timber buildings. However, at Heathrow postholes mark the site of a Celtic temple in a place

89 *The remains of the Romano-Celtic temple Maiden Castle (Dorset), as they appear today looking north-west. (See also* **colour plate 13**.)

that was not adapted into a Roman cult centre (see **8**). At Hayling Island a circular Iron Age temple has been identified beneath the circular stone temple of Roman date which was built during the first century, perhaps in connection with the contemporary major house at nearby Fishbourne (**90**). At Harlow (Essex) a recent excavation of the temple site has shown that the temple precinct contains Bronze Age cremations as well as evidence of Iron Age activity (see **9**). At most other temple sites similar concentrations of coins and brooches are usually the only surviving evidence of pre-Roman cult activity.

The development of pre-Roman cult centres into thriving temple sites during the Roman period is a phenomenon found throughout the province and elsewhere in the Empire. There were two basic reasons for this process. Firstly there was the political and social importance of creating a working amalgamation of Roman and Celtic cultures. Not only did this make for a more peaceable way of life but it also made it easier to manipulate and control the indigenous peoples. The Boudican Revolt had almost certainly been partly provoked by priests – the Temple of Claudius at Colchester was a prime target of the rebellion and much of the killing bore hallmarks of sacrifice and ritualistic mutilation. Crushing obscure cults carried on in remote bogs and forests was essential to the

destruction of the spiritual energy behind armed resistance.

Secondly there were the simple circumstances of places being brought into the infrastructure of a developing province, with its network of roads, navigable rivers, towns and other settlements. This meant that there were now people moving about, probably on a greater scale than there had ever been before, along with a much greater circulation of goods and other commodities. Shrines which lay on or close to major routes were bound to benefit from travellers passing by, which would in turn enhance the place's reputation.

In most cases the Roman temples which were built in countryside locations were in 'Romano-Celtic' form, though examples are also found within towns. In plan the type is extremely simple though there are many variations. The temples had a central square *cella* which contained the cult statue or statues, surrounded by a concentric square ambulatory. Often this basic design was modified, perhaps by divisions in the ambulatory or by the addition of external chambers to the ambulatory, for example the hill-top temple at Lamyatt Beacon (see **94**) (Somerset). The probable original appearance of such buildings has been deduced from the substantial remains of the Temple of Janus at Autun in France, which retains enough traces of the position of roofing timbers to make a reconstruction possible. Classical temples are to all intents and purposes unknown in the Romano-British countryside. There were other types: the circular temple at Hayling Island is

90 *Hayling Island temple (Hampshire) as it may have appeared in the later first century.*

one such instance, but even elaborate designs such as the octagonal temple at Nettleton retained the basic format of a central cella and external ambulatory.

Nettleton is an excellent place to start looking at how a site might develop as a result of its religious significance and physical location (see **88** and **colour plate 14**). It was one of several places which attracted attention shortly after the Roman Conquest because of its pre-Roman significance. Nettleton lies on the Fosse Way, the main route between Lincoln and Exeter, in a small secluded valley (**colour plate 14**). By about 47 a fort was built on the high ground immediately to the south, around the time that the road was serving as an early frontier.

Whether the fort was built because the valley already served as a cult centre or was just an area of native settlement is not known, but by the Flavian period a small circular shrine had been built on the slope overlooking the south bank of the river about 100m (330ft) from where the Fosse Way crossed it. Gradually other buildings were put up in the vicinity, so it seems that as the southern part of the province became stable Nettleton was able to enjoy the benefits of lying on a major route. With Bath only being about 16km (10 miles) to the south, and Cirencester 33km (20 miles) to the north it must have been a convenient overnight stop.

By the early years of the third century the cult had benefited so much that the temple was enhanced with an octagonal podium. Disaster

struck soon afterwards and the temple burnt down. However, the opportunity was taken to reconstruct the temple in a complicated octagonal form on the new podium (see **88**). The building probably resembled the sixth-century church of San Vitale at Ravenna in Italy which has a very similar plan. Unfortunately the architect's ambitions exceeded his skill because he omitted to make provision for the lateral forces created by the central part of the building. Despite some internal alterations to make good the lack of strength the temple eventually partly collapsed by the middle years of the fourth century.

Before this happened the site was obviously doing rather well. An altar and a plaque (see **86**) show that the temple was dedicated to Apollo associated with a Celtic deity called Cunomaglos. Cunomaglos is a Celtic name which means something like 'hound-prince' and as he is unknown from anywhere else it seems almost certain that this was the centre of his pre-Roman cult. The site has been quite widely excavated and there were evidently several buildings scattered about in the small valley. Some would have been used for housing pilgrims, others would have been occupied by the resident priests. One building was attached to the octagonal podium and stretched to the river bank. It may have been a meeting place for devotees of the cult but could also have been used for the purposes of bathing in the river in proximity to the god. There was also at least one other temple. The attractive location on a main road means that we don't necessarily have to interpret this as a wholly religious

107

place – for people living in nearby towns, Nettleton may also have acted as a pleasant recreational facility.

None the less, by about 330 Nettleton had ceased to act primarily as a cult centre. The damaged temple was allowed to deteriorate further and the place became a centre for manufacturing pewter. The alloy became popular in the fourth century, replacing good quality pottery and glassware for table use in households which could not afford silver. The temple's inherently poor design may have contributed to a decision to let it decay. It is equally possible, however, that the proximity of the much more imposing temple and associated cult structures at Bath was responsible, or that the increased popularity of Christianity had diminished the numbers of visitors. Towards the end of the fourth century the ruined temple was briefly adapted to accommodate some religious activity but by the end of the period the ruins had been incorporated into a farmstead. To some extent Nettleton parallels the country villas. A long period of modest existence was followed by a period of substantial capital investment in the later third and fourth centuries which was itself followed by decline, though here the decline preceded that found at most of the villas.

Nettleton had the advantage of passing trade, but there are many other examples of more remote rural temple sites. The temple at Harlow (Essex) was certainly the centre of an Iron Age cult (see 9). The focal point was a small hill in a river valley. By the end of the first century a Romano-Celtic temple of conventional design had been erected over the Iron Age site. Eventually an area in front of the temple was enclosed with a timber palisade. By the early third century this palisade was replaced with a stone wall to create two distinct but adjacent rectangular areas (91). The temple lay within the northern enclosure but was built up to the dividing wall through which access was possible from the southern enclosure. The actual altar lay on the central axis at the entrance. The southern enclosure had rectangular chambers built along its side walls and was itself reached through an imposing entrance, again on the main axis.

What had been a haphazard pre-Roman cult site had been replaced by an architecturally unsophisticated but symmetrical complex of buildings based on the temple structure. This is an interesting contrast with Nettleton, which by comparison was a straggling jumble of different buildings. The temple seems to have been dedicated to a number of different cults because a head of Minerva was found as well as a fragmentary altar which appears to refer to the emperor cult, and a carving of an anonymous Celtic warrior god. The site actually lies only about 32km (20 miles) from London and Verulamium but access seems to have been from a minor road to the north. There is little trace of rural settlement in the form of villas in the vicinity so the temple would only have been visited by people making a deliberate plan to do so. Nevertheless, the numbers of small finds from the site and the building work suggest that it was popular. But like the Nettleton temple the site had fallen into disuse by the mid-fourth century, though it seems to have been demolished instead of deteriorating, pointing once more to a possible decline in the popularity of rural cult centres. The temple at Hayling Island, also with a certain pre-Roman cult on the site had fallen into disuse by the early third century.

At some other sites cult activity went on much later, though in a few cases it had also started later. This is particularly true at Lydney Park (92) and Lamyatt Beacon. Lydney was not developed into a cult centre until the late third century at the earliest but the fact that it was dedicated to a little-known Celtic god called Nodens makes it likely that there was some sort of long-established local tradition of worshipping the god there, unless he was 'imported' from Ireland, which has been suggested. In fact the site was originally near a small Iron Age hillfort which overlooked the Severn Estuary and was used for the first part

91 (Right, above) *Reconstructed isometric view of the temple and precinct at Harlow (Essex) as it may have appeared in its fully developed form in the third century. The Romano-Celtic temple has been extended to join a wall which divided the precinct into two distinct areas. (See also* **9**.)

92 (Right, below) *Reconstructed view of the temple site at Lydney Park (Gloucestershire), dedicated to the god Nodens as it may have appeared during the fourth century. The temple stands in isolation surrounded by various buildings which were probably occupied by pilgrims. (After Wheeler, with alterations.)*

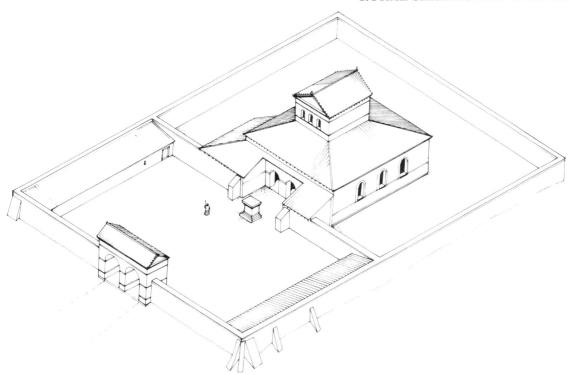

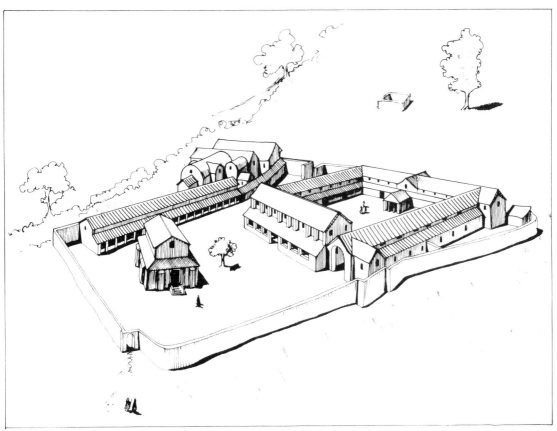

of the Roman period as a source of iron ore. The site is in a charming wooded location even today but despite its intimate setting it lay very close to the main road running between the *colonia* at Gloucester and the cantonal capital of the Silures at Caerwent and must have benefited accordingly.

Nodens was a truly Celtic deity and no known representation of him in human form has been found, so he probably retained some of the mystic aura which other Celtic gods may have lost during the Roman period. This could even have been an attraction to those concerned with reviving the cult, though he is known to have been associated with Mars and Silvanus. He was a healing and hunting god, a particularly popular type of deity. At least nine figures of dogs were found at the site. Nodens may have been perceived in dog form, but dogs are known to have been used in healing cults to lick wounds and other diseased parts of bodies elsewhere in the ancient world.

Healing cults required slightly more extensive facilities than simply a temple and a place to stay. The complex of buildings at Lydney included one which resembled a courtyard villa and would have been used for accommodation, a bath-house, and a range of individual rooms alongside the temple. The temple was designed by an architect who failed to notice that the site had a large fault in the rock immediately beneath one of the central piers. It collapsed and the temple had to be entirely rebuilt to a modified design. This was clearly intended to provide private niches and seats around the ambulatory which may have been for the benefit of pilgrims to sleep in the temple and make contact with the god through their dreams (**93**). A mosaic, now lost, from the floor of the temple bore an inscription referring to the presence on the site of one Victorinus the 'interpreter', probably of dreams.

Lamyatt Beacon is a hill in Somerset about 8km (5 miles) east of the Fosse Way. At some time in the late third century a fairly conventional Romano-Celtic temple was built there, though it had ante-chambers (**94**). Like Nettleton there seems only to be a tenuous connection with pre-Roman cults and certainly none of the direct continuity observed elsewhere. A number of classical gods were apparently worshipped, including Jupiter, Mars, Mercury, Minerva and a Genius, though Mars seems to have been pre-eminent. Interestingly this is

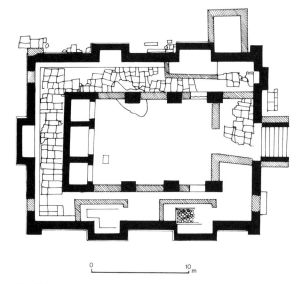

93 *Plan of the temple of Nodens at Lydney Park. Solid walls indicate the temple as originally designed. Hatched walls indicate sections introduced following a serious collapse of the structure when a pier fell into a natural fault around the year 370. (After Wheeler.)*

one of the few places where there is some indication of continuity into the post-Roman period. A small cemetery of the sixth to eighth centuries lay just to the north of the temple, possibly associated with a very small single-roomed building just by the temple. There may have been a small Christian monastic community at this date, something which was certainly encouraged by the Church which exploited the existence of traditional religious sites.

A small temple was built during the late fourth century on the hillfort of Maiden Castle (Dorset) (see **89** and **colour plate 13**). During excavation no obvious evidence for there having been a pre-Roman cult on the exact site of the temple was found, but the general location may have been regarded as sufficient. The temple had one simple building nearby, perhaps the priest's house, but traces of another structure, a round building, a little further off, around which a number of religious artefacts were found, have been interpreted as the remains of the temple 'shop'; literally a place where pilgrims might buy religious trinkets and curios. However, it could have been another temple as it overlies a pre-Roman building. Of course Maiden Castle lies only a

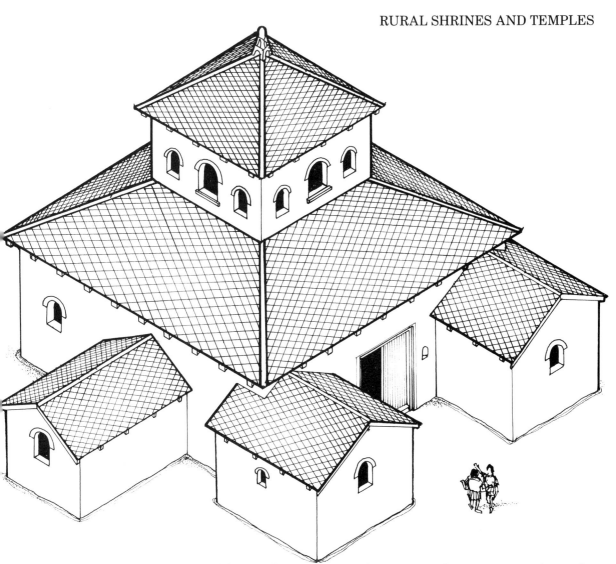

94 *Reconstructed isometric view of the temple at Lamyatt Beacon (Somerset). Built in the late third century and used up to the early fifth. The temple was relatively unusual in having three additional rooms, that on the left having a sunken floor (its precise form is uncertain).*

few miles from the Roman town at Dorchester, *Durnovaria*. The site is stunning and has excellent views. Whatever the religious significance of the place its late development creates the impression that this was as much an entrepreneurial establishment as anything else. Several deities were worshipped here on the evidence of the small finds, including Minerva and Diana, and a Celtic bull-god called Taurus Trigaranus. No doubt the temple and its location were regarded as a local sight, with the Durnova-

rians taking great pleasure in a trek up the hillside to the temple.

All temples except the poorest would have had some sort of stored wealth in the form of priestly regalia (**95**), and plate made from bronze (perhaps gilded or inlaid), silver or gold. It is hardly surprising that these are almost entirely absent from the archaeological record. However, the truly exceptional treasure found at Thetford (Norfolk) included silver spoons and jewellery buried on a site known to have been used as a high status religious centre in the pre-Roman period. The treasure is, however, fourth century in date and the spoons bear inscriptions stating that they belong to an obscure Italian rural god called Faunus (**96**, **colour plate 15**). The spoons would have been used by the members of the cult, some of whom

111

95 *Priest's lifesize bronze crown from a rural religious site at Hockwold-cum-Wilton (Norfolk).*

96 *One of the 33 silver spoons which formed part of the late fourth-century treasure from Thetford (Norfolk), associated with the god Faunus.* (British Museum.)

are also mentioned on the spoons, during ritual feasts. It is quite possible that a fourth-century temple lay close by though the site is now buried under an industrial building. The treasure itself was found by chance by a metal-detector user so it is possible that other temple sites may yet yield some of their wealthier possessions.

At all these places religious dedications were made by visitors; however, these did not have to be made at temples. Sometimes a simple open air shrine sufficed. One lay outside the Mithraeum at the fort of Carrawburgh on Hadrian's Wall. It was dedicated to local nymphs and the spirit (*genius*) of the place and consisted of little more than a semicircular seat with an altar and a well (97). Here offerings were made to the nymphs. Only a few yards away lay the spring dedicated to the goddess Coventina. When the spring was dug out in the nineteenth century it was found to contain thousands of coins and other gifts to the goddess (see 33).

There would have been shrines like this all over the province but naturally they have almost all vanished except in very remote places. Up on Scargill Moor near Bowes (Durham) two shrines lay close to one another. Altars found there were dedicated by soldiers from the nearby fort at Bowes to Vinotunus, a Celtic god associated with Silvanus, the Roman

god of woodlands and hunting (see also 31 for a similar example). Close to the fort at Risingham, north of Hadrian's Wall, lie the remains of a relief carved into the living rock. The relief depicts the lower half of a hunting god, probably Cocidius (the upper half was destroyed in the nineteenth century), and it too would have been the recipient of gifts and sacrifices by hunters (see 10). Even more obscure is the small carved relief of a warrior god carved into the rock at Yardhope, north of Hadrian's Wall, probably also a representation of Cocidius.

Among the minor settlements along the Fosse Way was one at Lower Slaughter (Gloucestershire). Although no temple is known there is some evidence for there being a small open air shrine. A number of carved stone reliefs depicting Celtic gods like the anonymous hooded trio, the *genii cucullati*, were found buried in a well. Two others may have depicted Minerva and a local variant of Mars respectively. All were heavily weathered and damaged which suggests that they were set up as offerings at a roadside shrine, perhaps represented by fragments of columns amongst the group. However, one of the representations of the hooded trio is clearly an incomplete rough-out so they may in fact have come from a sculptor's workshop. These carvings were probably mass-produced for sale, and not necessarily by skilled sculptors – Cotswold stone is extremely easy to carve and the present author was able to produce a perfectly respectable group of *genii* in under one hour having never carved before. The surviving examples are almost certainly a minute proportion of the number manufactured originally at the site, reflecting the softness of the limestone. It is therefore not surprising that the Cotswold area

97 *Plan of the* nymphaeum *just outside the entrance of the* mithraeum *close to the fort of Carrawburgh on Hadrian's Wall. The shrine consisted of little more than a semicircular stone seat and an altar dedicated to the nymphs, and was probably of typical of thousands of other lost examples.* (After Smith.)

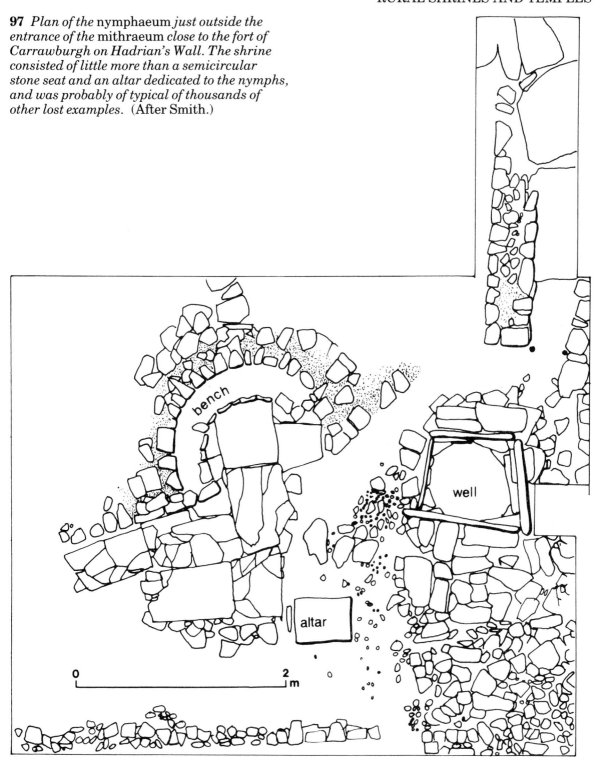

bench

well

altar

0   2 m

as a whole has probably produced more reliefs of a religious nature than any other part of the civilian province. We should be wary of attributing too much significance to individual examples because they are just as much a reflection of a rural industry as they are of cults.

Religion in the villas

In the Roman world all houses contained artefacts which were connected with religion. Whether these were incidental or fundamental to the house's existence is not quite so clear. Much the most vigorous source of debate is the mosaic flooring found in so many of the great country houses of the late third and fourth centuries. These floors almost invariably contained some sort of mythical reference, generally a portayal of an incident such as Jupiter as a bull making off with Europa at Lullingstone (see **62** and **colour plate 5**) or the more famous series of mosaics depicting Orpheus and his associates at villas like Woodchester, or in the triconch hall at Littlecote (**98**). Even if a mosaic lacks such a precise reference it may contain elements known to be attributes of a god, or animals associated with one. Occasionally it has been argued that mosaic floors contain discrete references to Christianity, and in the case of the Hinton St Mary mosaic which actually portrays the head of Christ, this is beyond doubt (**colour plate 16**).

These mosaics are exceedingly hard to interpret satisfactorily. In many cases the religious reference is fairly clear but we cannot discern whether the mosaic's topic reflected the purpose of either the room or even the building. Were the Orphic mosaics in rooms used for the observation of Orphic cults by gatherings of the faithful? Or were they simply laid because Orphic designs were regarded as attractive and were popular as a result? They generally include some sort of circle of animals marching about the floor with Orpheus (see **47**). This undoubtedly diminished the usual disadvantage of more conventional mosaics which can only be properly observed from one side. At Woodchester, columns in the floor suggest that there was some sort of upstairs gallery from which the mosaic could be viewed to maximum advantage. This means that there must have been an element of pure ostentation in having the floor.

The mosaic at Thruxton which names one

98 *Mosaic from the triconch hall at Littlecote (Wiltshire), as recorded in the eighteenth century. The restoration omits a small dog or fox by the central figure of Orpheus which has been incorporated into the re-laid floor.* (British Museum.)

Quintus Natalius Natalinus is incomplete but the latter part of the inscription appears to have included the word '*voto*' (see **61**). A '*votum*' was a vow, normally a vow to a god. As the mosaic's central feature was a figure of Bacchus, the mosaic was probably laid to fulfil a promise to that god. At least that is nominally what appears to have happened. Whether there was really any meaningful cultic significance is quite another matter. The problem with mosaics is knowing whether their topics were merely conventional portrayals of stock themes of whether they represent truly useful information about the beliefs of their owners.

One particularly complicating feature is the way in which some mosaics contain a number of apparently contradictory themes. The mosaic at Frampton (Dorset) is thought to have been laid by the same mosaicist responsible for the Hinton St Mary floor. It contains a 'Chi-Rho' symbol, a universal and unequivocal reference to Christianity. However, it also contains references to Neptune in the form of marine scenes and an epigram; Cupids, also with an epigram; and a stock depiction of good defeating evil in the form of Bellerophon killing the Chimaera. Bellerophon is also depicted at Hinton and Lullingstone and it has been suggested that the scene was being used as a Christian allegory.

None of this necessarily prevents us from believing that the occupants of Hinton and Frampton were operating house churches. In the Roman world it was normal, and even customary, to be flexible and eclectic towards different cults, and to select features which were perceived as attractive or appropriate to personal beliefs. But whether we can justifiably be certain of the existence of house churches at these places, on the basis of the evidence available, is quite another matter. The fact that they are exceptionally rare, and in Hinton's case unique, but close together and possibly laid by the same man, raises the plausible possibility that they represent a local fashion or trend, perhaps even promoted by a local mosaicist who offered these themes as his trademark. Unfortunately for us, the quality of the archaeological evidence is simply not adequate to draw a firm conclusion either way. At none of these places has any sort of artefactual equipment in the form of inscribed silver or pewter vessels been found which would support the case for the presence of a cult, of whatever kind. Bellerophon was not used as a Christian allegory very often in the rest of the Empire and at Lullingstone the floor was laid some time before the installation of the Christian wall-plaster in a separate (and self-contained) part of the house.

In a small number of cases, though, a more important religious status has been argued when the villa buildings are associated with temples. The major villa at Chedworth is one such instance. In its final, fourth-century, form the villa had two substantial bath-suites, a considerable number of rooms arranged in four wings and a small temple-like building with a pool (see **44**). Another possible temple lay nearby, though it is as likely to have been a mausoleum associated with the villa – the

99 *Badly weathered carving of a hunter-warrior god from Chedworth (Gloucestershire), perhaps Mars.*

evidence from the excavation is inconclusive. The recovery of a number of carved reliefs depicting hunting gods (**99**), one in the nearby temple, and references to the healing god Mars-Lenus has led to the suggestion that rather than being a villa this was actually a place more akin to somewhere like Lydney Park. But the evidence is not conclusive because there is no temple which acts as central feature of the site. The nearby temple may have served as shrine to Mars-Lenus, and this may have had pre-Roman connections, but it is just as possible that the villa owner capitalized on this fortunate coincidence and exploited the shrine as a 'side-line' to the estate, accommodating paying visitors. There is certainly no reason to assume that Chedworth was not the centre of a large estate with agricultural activities as well, or perhaps the country residence of a wealthy family who enjoyed high status in provincial government at Cirencester, only 12km (7 miles) to the south – from the late third century Cirencester served as a provincial capital when Britain was sub-divided into four provinces.

The various candidates for religious buildings associated with villas may possibly have been a result of fourth-century official repression of paganism, particularly in the towns. In architectural terms the Littlecote hall is one of the most striking appendages to a villa building (see **48** and **colour plate 2**). In many of the towns evidence for the practice of paganism diminishes during the fourth century, for instance the deliberate burial of the sculptures at the London *mithraeum*, the abandonment of the Verulamium theatre by the end of the fourth century (it was closely associated with a large Romano-Celtic temple and was almost certainly used for religious ceremonies), and also the 'Triangular Temple' at Verulamium which fell out of use during the fourth century. However most of the rest of Verulamium shows evidence for abandonment by this time, so this may merely be a reflection of demand. Perhaps pagan cults were likely only to flourish in the privacy of country estates or rural locations, but however mosaic floors are interpreted the only firm conclusion can be that they represent the interests of their owners; we cannot infer that they were therefore places in which cults were practised.

The kind of back garden, grotto-style, religion found at Chedworth was popular in the Roman world where the wealthy often fantasized about rural life, most commonly expressed in the form of wall-paintings depicting romantic, mythological and bucolic scenes. The villa of Herodes Atticus just outside Rome no longer exists but a semi-subterranean grotto to Neptune in its garden complete with statue and spring can still be seen today. The religious reference is not in question but it was also a pretty place to sit. None of the surviving mosaics at Chedworth refer to Mars or Lenus and instead depict innocuous geometric themes – cupids, the Four Seasons and possibly Bacchus. So even if the place was a cult centre for Mars-Lenus it was evidently not thought necessary to refer to the fact on the mosaic floors, which raises more doubts about the validity of deducing the presence of a cult on the basis of floor motifs at other places.

Several other villas fall into this curious category of houses which are thought to have perhaps had other purposes: Great Witcombe (Gloucestershire) (**100**), Lufton (Somerset) (see **49**) and Holcombe (Devon). The latter two had ostentatious and disproportionately sized bath-suites. Great Witcombe was built on a steep hillside over a spring (see **50**) and as at the other two, an excessive amount of the building seems given over to rooms which were not living quarters. But the evidence for cult activities is even more circumstantial than at Chedworth. These houses are just as likely to have been the product of whims and extravagance.

A few villas have yielded fragments of stone statuary like the marble figures of Bacchus from a grave near the villa at Spoonley Wood (see **63**) and a Diana Luna from Woodchester (Gloucestershire) (see **64**). These are exceptional, but all villas would have contained small statues and statuettes made out of bronze, fired clay or wood. They could represent mainstream deities like the bronze Minerva Victrix from Plaxtol (**101**), or spirits which were more directly identifiable with the owners. Such statuettes may well have been purchased from cult centres as souvenirs. A small bronze figure of Mercury from the Uley temple may have been intended for sale (**102**). In romanized households these would have been displayed in a small shrine, the *lararium*, alongside representations of family antecedents but Lullingstone is the only place in Britain to have produced ancestor busts carved in marble and obviously of considerable value (see **60**). Lullingstone's second-century painting of water nymphs probably referred to the river which runs only a few metres away: they represented a personification of the river spirits (**colour plate 11**).

Lullingstone's third-century owners continued to revere the busts. By the late fourth century their descendants or new owners were engaged in patronizing a relatively new cult in part of their house apparently given over to Christianity. The installation of wall-paintings depicting figures engaged in worship along with Christian symbols makes this likely (**103**). But perhaps the same points made about mosaics above could apply here too. No artefacts associated with worship were found, so possibly the paintings were purely decorative. But depiction of the people worshipping is emphatic and straightforward, there is no vague allegorical tone; moreover the construction of a Saxon church a few yards away at a

100 *Part of the south wing of the villa at Great Witcombe (Gloucestershire), as it appears today. The presence of a font and three niches may mean that this was a domestic shrine.*

later date does point to a folk memory that this was once a place for Christian worship. The excavator was of the opinion that the 'Christian' rooms were self-contained and separate from the rest of the house and this reinforces the possibility that this was indeed a house-church.

If Christianity did have an active presence at Lullingstone it is an exceptionally rare instance of an eastern 'mystery' religion having a presence in the Romano-British countryside. Normally cults such as that of Mithras only functioned in an urban or military setting where an influx of people from abroad both introduced and sustained the religion. One possible *mithraeum* was found at Burham (Kent) but no artefactual evidence was found there to

101 *Bronze figure of Minerva from the Alan's Farm villa, Plaxtol (Kent). Found during agricultural work in the mid-nineteenth century. Height 19cm (7½in).*

117

102 *Bronze figure of Mercury from Uley (Gloucestershire). Height 10cm (4in).* (British Museum.)

103 *Some of the fourth-century Christian wall-plaster from the villa at Lullingstone (Kent), which illustrates a number of figures engaged in what appears to be prayer.* (English Heritage.)

support this identification. In the Romano-British countryside it looks as if religion was deeply conservative. The Latin word *paganus* means literally a 'country dweller' and it is no coincidence that the Latin word was used by Christians as a disparaging term for people who subscribed to traditional religions. A number of lead tanks which bear Christian symbols have been found at several rural locations, for example a well-preserved example from Icklingham (Suffolk), the site of a small settlement (**104**). It is possible that they formed part of the equipment of itinerant priests, serving as baptismal fonts, and were taken around the province to those places where the priest was welcomed.

Death and burial in the countryside

On a hill-slope called Leafy Grove in west Kent a number of simple cremation burials dating to the late first or early second century were found in 1969. They lay some 25m (80ft) from what appears to have been a Romano-British farmstead (roof tiles and a quernstone were found) of the same date and almost certainly contained the remains of members of the family who worked the land from there.

The five burials which were excavated were all modest. The burnt remains were contained in vessels of a local coarse ware though at least two were accompanied by flagons and one of these also had a small samian cup. The site itself was probably abandoned by the second quarter of the second century but the modest burials are representative of thousands of other rural cremation finds which have been found throughout Britain. Unfortunately the nature of the cremations is such that we can usually

104 *Lead tank, probably a baptismal font, from Icklingham (Suffolk), bearing the Christian Chi-Rho monogram. The original tank was 1.8m (just under 6ft) in diameter.* (British Museum.)

tell very little about the people involved. But the pottery used to contain these people was of the cheapest and most easily obtainable type, though they had enough money to own some samian and a beaker or two which they could spare for a burial.

Close to the Leafy Grove site is a villa site at Keston. Although the villa is not visible today the remains of two mausolea are. They lie close to the villa and were undoubtedly used for members of the owner's family. Unlike the people at Leafy Grove these villa residents were prepared to invest more in the afterlife for at least one of their number. He, or she (though there may have been more than one), was interred in a substantial buttressed stone circular tomb originally up to 6m (20ft) in height, which was plastered and painted (105). Immediately next to this tomb is a smaller rectangular one which contained an inhumation in a stone coffin. A number of other burials have also been located in the immediate vicinity including a cremation sealed in a tile chamber built between two of the buttresses of the circular tomb.

Another feature of the remarkable Lullingstone site is the mausoleum built a few metres away from the villa house on the slope above (106). This tomb consisted of a central vaulted chamber with a subterranean compartment for the burials and some sort of external ambulatory. The excavator believed it was a temple as well as a mausoleum but no evidence for any sort of cult activity was found. The building was put up around the year 300 and contained a young woman and man interred in individual decorated lead coffins accompanied by a number of grave goods including a bronze flagon (107) glassware and games (108). The burials had been placed at the bottom of a shaft within a wooden chamber strengthened with iron bolts and angles. Layers of chalk and gravel had been packed on top of this up to ground level. Not surprisingly the weight of this spoil and the rotting of the wood caused the chamber to collapse, attracting the attention of late fourth-century tomb robbers who invaded the tomb and removed one of the coffins.

The history of the Lullingstone tomb is particularly interesting but it was obviously exceptional in the history of the house. Though other tombs must have existed, considering the length of time the building was occupied, none was placed so close to the house and in such a dominating position. No villa in Britain has ever been associated with a group of graves

105 *Tombs close to the villa site at Keston (Kent). The larger was probably once quite tall as it required buttressing. Other minor graves in the vicinity indicate that this was where members of the villa family were customarily buried.*

large enough to account for all the occupants likely to have lived there over a period of two or more centuries. While this must in part reflect the archaeological exploration of these sites it is possible that a proportion of people who lived in the countryside were actually buried in urban cemeteries. There has always been something of a problem in explaining the contradiction between the large inhumation cemeteries of the fourth centuries outside several major towns combined with a perceived decline in the density of urban occupation. The position from an archaeological perspective is very difficult and some of the problems were discussed in the companion volume to this one. Nevertheless there remains the possibility that there was some sort of social tradition of being buried near a town.

106 *Bronze jug from the mausoleum at Lullingstone (Kent). The cap is attached by a chain. No later than about 300 and about 21cm (8¼in) high. (English Heritage.)*

Much the most poignant feature of death in the countryside was the burial of infants. It was not uncommon to bury babies which had miscarried or died shortly after birth within a building, sometimes as a kind of foundation deposit. Lullingstone contained one cut into the concrete floor of a room some time in the late fourth century. Accompanied by grave goods the manner of the child's burial was clearly pagan in tone, yet this was the time when the house was possibly acting as a Christian house-church too. At other places the burial of babies may be linked to the disposal of unwanted slave offspring (see p.83).

107 (Above) *Bone disc from the villa site at Lullingstone (Kent), depicting either Medusa or a goddess. Probably cut down from a larger plaque to make a gaming piece, the disc was found placed on a coffin in the mausoleum close to the villa. Representations of Medusa are known on other coffins and there are mythological associations – her blood was thought to have been able to revive the dead. Diameter 3.2cm (1.¹/₄in), c. 300. (English Heritage.)*

108 *Reconstructed isometric view of the villa at Lullingstone, as it may have appeared at its height during the latter part of the fourth century. The mausoleum just above later became the site of a small Saxon church, perhaps indicating that the presence of a Roman house church at the villa had endured in local folklore.*

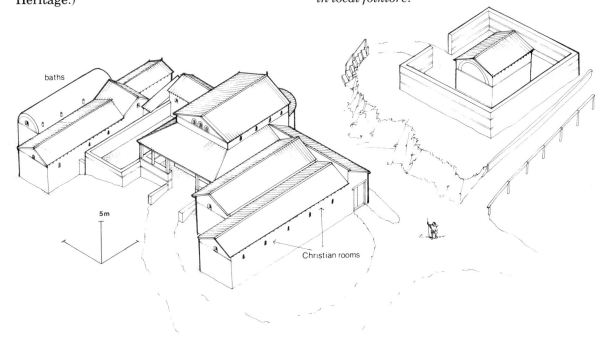

baths

5m

Christian rooms

8

Change and continuity in the fifth century

It is very easy to see the end of Roman Britain as exclusively a time of change. The very limited historical evidence we possess paints such a picture and much of the archaeological record exhibits an abrupt end to both the enormous quantities of artefacts and the occupation of structures so typical of Roman sites. In a political sense the end of Britain's official connection with the Roman world is taken to be around the year 410, following the ejection of Roman officials in 409 and the Emperor Honorius' subsequent advice to the Romano-British cities to take care of their own defence. It is very easy to assume that this was a cataclysmic time which affected every part of the community and economy.

The truth of course is that most of the population, and this applies especially to the countryside, would almost certainly have continued their lives without very much practical disruption. People still needed food and they still needed to have somewhere to live. The majority of the Romano-British occupied modest farmsteads in the countryside. Even during the Roman period these places had relatively limited access to manufactured goods like fine pottery, and this makes them difficult to date and analyse. By the time that Roman government had ceased to be of significance these sites have become virtually undatable. This makes it very difficult to be sure which places were occupied in the fifth century, and therefore to assess whether the population of the countryside as a whole was declining, expanding or remaining static. There are some regional examples where wholesale abandonment of settlements suggests local movements and decline. In the Upper Thames area Romano-British settlements were widely distributed across the river valley. Before the end of the fifth century they were no longer occupied and associated drainage systems had been abandoned. Settlement instead moved to the slightly higher ground which did not require so much maintenance – the implication is that there was less demand for land.

The nature of the political upheavals and the barbarian incursions into the northern part of the Roman Empire in the fourth and fifth centuries encourages us to associate archaeological changes with these events. However, other factors which cannot be identified so easily may have been involved, for example disease. The sixth-century chronicler Gildas recorded a catastrophic plague in Britain in the fifth century, though typically it is presented as a divine punishment for excessive good living following a decline in barbarian raiding; we cannot know if the plague's effect on the population was as dramatic as he described. The importance is more that it reminds us that all human communities suffer devastating losses from the episodic appearance of new diseases and that these losses are usually just as great as the effects of war, and can have a significant impact on settlement.

Throughout the Roman period the towns contained the largest quantities of the manufactured goods and fittings which we regard as the definitive features of the Roman world. Their decline is thus a measure of the decline of romanization. All the towns, large and small, demonstrate a marked decline in the quality and density of occupation during the fifth century. In some towns where continuity has been identified, and Verulamium is one of the best examples, it is confined to a very small proportion of the examined sites. In other words, most of the excavated plots do not show any evidence for continuity.

In the countryside the evidence for decline is, if anything, more acute, or to look at it another way the disappearance of evidence which we use as a measure of Romanization is more noticeable – but then there was less of it to begin with; Roman towns always produce proportionally far more artefacts than Roman rural sites, so the disappearance of artefacts is therefore all the more pronounced. Rubbish was usually buried in pits in or around urban buildings, or consolidated into rubble as a site was levelled for rebuilding. On rural sites this was obviously neither desirable nor necessary – rubbish could be buried at some distance – and as excavations tend to concentrate on structures then rubbish is not so easily recovered other than in more exceptional circumstances (see the Plaxtol samian bowl, **82**).

Many individual villas will have experienced episodes of decline or abandonment throughout the Roman period. These periods are often observed in the archaeological record and may have lasted several decades, for example at Llantwit Major or Lullingstone, where the houses seem to have been left vacant for part of the third century. As nothing is known of Romano-British villa ownership or the history of a single household we have to consider many different possible reasons. A villa owner could have had his property seized by the government for treasonable activities, he may have had to sell his estate to settle debts or the house may have become too expensive to repair.

Nevertheless, for the most part such villas were eventually renovated and restored. These incidents were all part of a normal cycle of change but whatever happened they show that while they were being repaired and maintained villas had a part in the social and economic structure of the province. The villas were where the wealthy members of the population, at least in part, spent their money. The money was mostly earned by selling the surplus products of successful agriculture, almost certainly in towns. They also supported towns through their demand for access to manufactured goods, either imported or made in Roman Britain. The largest number of villas were in existence during the fourth century and a significant proportion were expensively decorated and equipped.

By about 375 this situation had been transformed. While many of the villas continued in use, those which were abandoned were not reoccupied. Equally significantly no new ones were built. We have already seen that the villa at Gadebridge Park was not only abandoned but comprehensively demolished too, well before the end of the fourth century. Lullingstone had been burnt down by the early part of the fifth century and that was the end of the house's existence. The natural erosion of the steep hillside above it covered the ruins and, apart from the Saxon church which was built there, the site disappeared (see **108**).

At other places where occupation did not immediately cease a marked decline in the quality of villa life is sometimes found, so-called 'squatter' occupation. This implies that the house was abandoned and had been reoccupied by degenerate vagrants. However, the occupants cannot be distinguished and it is possible that the same people were living there but in an impoverished state. At Keynsham (Avon) the house was damaged by fire but occupation continued, though the residents now laid hearths over the old mosaics. At Latimer (Buckinghamshire) fewer rooms seem to have been occupied, though occupation may have continued well into the fifth century at this level.

A reduction in house size was more certainly the case at Redlands Farm, Stanwick. Here the simple house had originally been enlarged by the expedient of adding two flanking wings to the rectangular main block (see **52**). Structural difficulties with the wings led to their demolition in the late fourth century. They were not replaced. Within the rest of the house the hypocaust was allowed to crumble beyond repair and the mosaic floors were cleared away, their *tesserae* being dumped to one side of the surviving rooms. Obviously the owners had neither the inclination nor the funds to repair the house, even though someone was still living there. Even at Lullingstone, where the Christian rooms were in use during the late fourth century, the bath-suite had long since been abandoned.

If the villa houses were being allowed to decay it is wrong to assume that therefore the associated land was no longer being worked. It is quite possible that the farming activities were continuing. After all, the population still needed food. We might consider modern parallels where landowners continue to manage and run their estates but cannot afford the upkeep

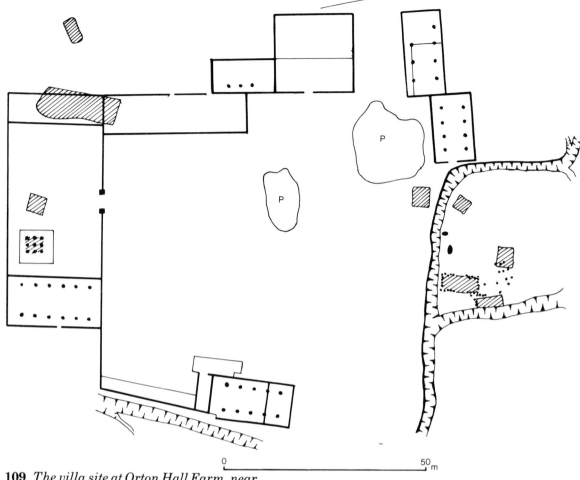

109 *The villa site at Orton Hall Farm, near Peterborough (Cambridgeshire), showing the location of Saxon settlement within and around the Roman structures and enclosures (hatched). (After Mackreth.)*

of the grand houses which were built in the eighteenth and nineteenth centuries. The difference in the late Roman period was that a reduction of the population dependent on food produced by others (i.e. the military and urban populations) would have meant that there was no longer any point in sustaining production at high levels. Not only did surplus production disappear but so also did the wealth earned from it. The market for it had diminished so naturally the supply did too.

Where this cycle began we cannot say but it follows that if a component is removed or becomes reduced then the whole economic edifice will crumble. So the villas and their owners withdrew into their own small-scale self-

sufficient units – or to look at it another way the gap between them and the traditional farmsteads had closed. That 'gap', both economic and social, had only been created as a result of forming part of the Roman world. In a small number of instances evidence has been identified for the actual estates being worked after the decay of the villa house. At Frocester (Gloucestershire) part of the villa house had burnt down by the early fifth century. It was not replaced but the rest of the house remained in use, and its garden remained in cultivation. At Orton Hall Farm near Peterborough some of the former villa buildings were either adapted or overlain by structures of Saxon date (**109**).

Identifying continuity of the estates in terms of their boundaries is much more difficult. There are several instances in Gaul where the old villa estates remained in use and their Roman identity was sustained. During the fifth century one Sidonius Apollinaris wrote an account of his villa estate, complete with baths, at Avitacum. In the sixth century the bishop of Trier, Nicetius, had a villa with associated farming activities. In Britain, however, continuity seems almost invariably to have been of a much more down-market nature. It is possible to try and form links between natural features, parish boundaries and villas. At Withington (Gloucestershire) a self-contained valley may correspond to the old villa estate. At Ditchley (Oxfordshire) not only do some earthworks and woodland seem to form a perimeter around the villa estate but a surviving footpath leads from the Roman road of Akeman Street directly towards the site of the Roman house. This certainly suggests the partial survival of evidence for a land unit.

Obviously the tendency is to locate only sites where occupation did not continue. Some medieval farms can be associated with farmsteads mentioned in the Domesday Book. Some of these are still farms. There may be some unlocated villa sites which have remained buried beneath farms which have been in more or less continuous occupation since antiquity. Even monasteries and their lands may conceal villa estates, where an attraction had been some sort of religious association. At Montcaret in the Dordogne in Gaul a substantial villa did not survive into the post-Roman period but was swiftly built over by a religious complex which is itself built over by a still extant church. In Britain there are no such elaborate examples but we might consider the church which lies over the major villa at Woodchester, the Saxon church which sat over the 'Temple-Mausoleum' at Lullingstone, or the small chapel which was built over a room in a villa at Widford (Oxfordshire) (the mosaic floor is still partly visible today). All these instances may be cases of villa estates which had survived into the medieval period being absorbed by the powerful medieval church.

An interesting feature of the late Roman period in Britain is the increase in the number of unrecovered rural hoards, of both coin and plate. Hoarding is a routine way of safeguarding wealth in any society without a developed banking system. It need not necessarily indicate a time of 'crisis' because the wealth was best placed out of sight all the time. But hoarding does increase at a time of insecurity – though the only evidence for that is an increase in the number of hoards which were not

recovered by their owners, and which have since been found. While for the most part this may be attributable (though not demonstrably) to innocuous reasons, a protracted period of insecurity might either result in the death of a larger number of hoarders either because they were killed, or because the time went on so long that they died before they felt safe to recover it. Naturally, we have no idea of the numbers of hoards which were recovered.

Stylistic analysis of the Mildenhall treasure has led to the suggestion that it was buried after the year 360 (see **43**). Unfortunately ownership cannot be attributed to any one individual though attempts have been made to link it with the family or associates of one Lupicinus. Lupicinus was a general despatched to Britain in 360 to deal with trouble on the northern frontier. While he was away Julian (360–3) was declared Emperor while the legitimate Emperor, Constantius II, was fighting in the East. Julian had Lupicinus arrested on his return, fearing that he would oppose his untimely elevation.

Like so many attempts to link artefacts or buildings with known and colourful events there is no basis for associating the Mildenhall hoard with Lupicinus, even if the plate was of exceptional quality and richness. The hoard could date much later than saying '360 or after' implies. But then it is only exceptional by our standards because there is so little like it. Considering how extravagant some of the late villas were, perhaps we should think in terms of this being normal for wealthy villa owners who, as conditions deteriorated, panicked over what to do with their stores of treasures. Other hoards known from Scotland (Traprain) and Ireland (Coleraine) show that silver was finding its way into barbarian hands, either because it was stolen or because it was handed over in an attempt to buy off raiders. A wealthy villa owner would have been keen to prevent his silver disappearing with raiders, or with officials seizing it for bribing barbarians. Unfortunately the find-spot, near Mildenhall in Suffolk, was inconclusive. A small fourth-century building seems to have existed nearby but there are relatively few villas in the area, lying on the edge of the Fens.

Curiously the other most important hoards of similar date were also found in East Anglia. At Thetford the circumstantial association with a pre-Roman settlement site, possibly of tribal significance, together with references on the finds themselves make it more likely that it was associated with a temple. The Thetford treasure was made up of 22 gold rings (**colour plate 15**), a belt buckle, four bracelets, several pendants and necklaces, 33 silver spoons (see **96**) and three strainers. The spoons bear unequivocal references to a cult of Faunus, an obscure Latin deity associated with Pan, and indicate the existence of a small group of people seeking security through the retrospective worship of an old cult which was unadulterated by corruption or assocations with Christianity. Likely to be late fourth century, or even later, the failure to recover such an amount of valuable material is difficult to explain. Perhaps the cult was actively suppressed or the climate of insecurity discouraged its removal.

In 1992 an even more remarkable discovery was made at Hoxne, near Eye, Suffolk. The find consisted of a substantial quantity of gold jewellery, silver plate and approximately 14,000 gold coins. Some of the silver pieces bear inscriptions which make it certain the hoard was Christian; however, there are no known Roman buildings in the vicinity, making its origins obscure, particularly as the coins date its deposition to after 411. It may have been owned by a Christian community based in either a villa or a town, whose members hid the treasure. Why it was never recovered can only remain a mystery, but the reason is likely to be linked to the increasing disorder of the period.

Hoards of silver coins of late date are also more common in Britain than elsewhere in the Empire, with the dates of the latest coins (which therefore give the earliest date for the hoard) being generally around the beginning of the fifth century. These consist mainly of silver *siliquae* of the Emperors Arcadius and Honorius, struck at Milan after the year 395. Coinage ceased to be supplied to Britain shortly after the beginning of the fifth century. Instead of making do with locally-produced copies (as had been a routine practice during earlier interruptions in supply, which itself demonstrates that the economy required coin) coinage began gradually to disappear altogether from Roman Britain. In the countryside this was almost total. Quality coinage was largely withdrawn into hoards. The logical conclusion is that there was no functioning economy which required the use of coins. Coinage had become exclusively a repository of wealth rather than a medium of exchange.

Once the coin supply had ceased silver which was still in circulation was increasingly subjected to clipping. These coins, known as 'clipped *siliquae*', had slivers of silver cut from their edges as the only remaining means of acquiring silver. Hoards of progressively later date can be partly identified through the increasing proportion of clipped coins. Clipping has been dated to various points in the early fifth century. It may have gone on a long time – with no new coins it is impossible to say. It is not a phenomenon found elsewhere on such a scale and its only effect can have been to destroy all confidence in what remained of the silver coinage.

For the Romano-British countryside the collapse of currency was another feature of the destruction of the economic base. For any establishment concerned with more than day-to-day subsistence the disappearance of coin meant a reversion to barter if the surplus was to be exchanged for anything. It meant the disruption of a sophisticated economy where manufactured goods were produced, transported and sold. The role of the merchant would have been destroyed and therefore also the middle ground of the workforce not primarily engaged in basic production. With the withdrawal of a formal administration and the decline of a centralized authority the taxation system collapsed too and that reduced the incentive to earn cash with which to pay taxes.

In all the industries of Roman Britain this can be seen happening towards the end of the fourth century and by the beginning of the fifth. The most conspicuous is the collapse of the pottery industries of the countryside. These were mainly the Oxfordshire and the Alice Holt potteries (see p.100). Although both industries worked from kiln sites dispersed across their respective regions, the distribution of their products was biased in favour of the towns. To put it another way more of their goods are found in towns, and in towns which were further away from the kiln sites than the rural areas which they reached. This was because the distribution was dependent on lines of communications; and of course the lines of communications passed through the towns.

Pottery was a fairly basic everyday commodity and most establishments would have had to spend some money on it most of the time, so it is an extremely important indicator of the dwindling state of Roman Britain. For the wealthy, however, there was a variety of ways in which wealth could be spent. It has already been noted that villa building ceased and so did the peripheral industries associated with it, like the laying of mosaics. It was also common for the aristocratic tier of Romano-British society to pay for the erection and dedication of temples. Although it is rare for us to be able to associate such philanthropic works to individuals the lost mosaic from Lydney stated that the floor had been laid by Titus Flavius Senilis out of offerings from pilgrims. The temple itself was a fairly new one and had only been built in the fourth century.

The Thetford Faunus cult was almost certainly a fourth-century revival, though the temple has not been located. Maiden Castle's modest temple was built on a fresh site in the fourth century within the old Iron Age hillfort (**colour plate 13**). The temple at Brean Down, overlooking the Bristol Channel, seems to have been built during the second quarter of the fourth century. During the fourth century the cult of Mercury at Uley (Gloucestershire) became centred on a new stone temple. This wave of temple-building has been seen, not unreasonably, as part of the villa-enlargement phenomenon of the fourth century. The temples were being built by villa owners as another way of spending their money, displaying their wealth and possibly even acting as a further source of income.

However, the temple-building had ceased by the end of the fourth century too. The temples generally became disused though there are isolated instances of possible continuity of venerated sites. At Nettleton the temple had collapsed due partly to a poorly executed design. By the end of the fourth century its ruins had been adapted to form part of a farmstead. Evidently there was neither the money nor the incentive to repair the elaborate structure. Lamyatt Beacon's temple site was accompanied by a small cemetery of sixth-century or later date and a small cell-like building, though the latter may be late Roman in date. Perhaps it had become the residence of a hermit, or a very small religious community.

One phenomenon found across the Roman Empire and in particular in the north-west provinces is the imposition of Christian churches on pagan sites. This was actively recommended by Pope Gregory in the year 601 in a letter to the Abbot Mellitus who was about to leave for Britain. Mellitus was advised to destroy images of pagan gods but to cleanse temples and adapt them for use as churches. In this way the people would be able to carry on worshipping in their accustomed places and with the skilful use of this positive psychology they would learn to worship the Christian God. Gildas, writing in the mid-sixth century, had commented on how places considered sacred by pagan cults were still being venerated. Although structural continuity has not been demonstrated anywhere there are several rural temple sites where new buildings replaced the old temples. At Uley the temple appears to have partly fallen down around 380 though it remained in use into the fifth century. Subsequently a church-like building was erected directly over the site. It may be of significance that

110 *Lifesize stone bust of Mercury from the villa at Uley (Gloucestershire), originally forming part of a complete statue. The head was buried in a purpose-built stone cist by the fifth century, around the time that the site may have been reused for a church. That it was treated with respect indicates that it was either too feared or revered to be destroyed. (British Museum.)*

the cult statue of Mercury's broken remains were buried beneath in the temple's ruins, the head being carefully placed in a specially built cist (**110**). Even if Mercury had had his day his image was still respected.

Although it seems increasingly that there was a level of rural continuity which sustained the agricultural base of Britain, it is not generally possible to be certain who was actually working the land in any one case. Were the fifth-century inhabitants of any particular locality the descendants of the local villa family? Or was the land actually being worked by immigrants from northern Europe? The emergence of pottery and building types typical of the Germanic peoples, particularly in the eastern part of Britain does point to this. We know from sources like Gildas and Bede that the Saxon peoples from northern Europe began to move into Britain in numbers from around the middle of the fifth century. There will have been earlier influxes which were not recorded and are difficult to discern in the archaeological record – artefacts are not necessarily proof of the movements of peoples, particularly when they are not numerous. However, the Germanic peoples had already been used as mercenary forces to help defend the island and they may ultimately have served as a 'fifth column' for the more systematic migrations of the later fifth century. It is clear that in succeeding decades the Saxons and Britons were engaged in sporadic warfare while the appearance of Saxon cemeteries along parts of the east coast shows that the Saxons had gained a foothold. There must have been a dispossession, or at least abandonment, of Romano-British farmsteads in the eastern part of Britain and Orton Hall Farm (see **109**) is probably one such instance.

The effect on the British seems to have been to encourage a withdrawal to the central and western part of Britain, in any case the more agriculturally fertile zone. A small number of sites in the west, such as South Cadbury and Tintagel, have indicated from their finds that they may have been occupied by people who had aspirations and contacts more in harmony with the wealthy occupants of the fourth-century villas. South Cadbury is a hill in Somerset; it has a long history and was originally an Iron Age hillfort. Some traces of first-century Roman military equipment suggest that it was one of the hillforts overwhelmed just after the

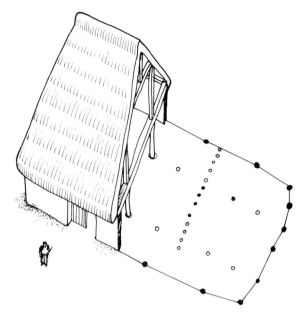

111 *Reconstructed cutaway axonometric view of a timber and thatched hall in occupation at South Cadbury in the fifth or sixth century. Dated by the presence of* amphorae *sherds. Approximately 19m (62ft) long and 10m (33ft) wide.* (Based on a plan by L. Alcock.)

Roman invasion. In the fifth century it was reoccupied; the rampart was repaired and a timber building erected within (**111**). Whoever was behind the reoccupation had access to trade routes which were quite out of context with the rest of Britain at that time. While the absence of pottery helps define other sites of the period, South Cadbury was receiving imports of foods and drink contained within *amphorae* originating in the Mediterranean lands. Fine pottery known now as African Red Slip Ware was also imported. This ware was a North African regional product which became popular around the Mediterranean, especially in the West, following the collapse of the samian industry. Clearly the residents of South Cadbury felt this kind of pottery was an important accessory and made sure that it was available to them. Considering the general collapse of the trading system it must have been relatively expensive and arduous to sustain such a contact. We have no idea what was used as payment – perhaps metals like tin, just as before the Conquest in 43.

Tintagel, a promontory on the north coast of Cornwall is another site which has produced

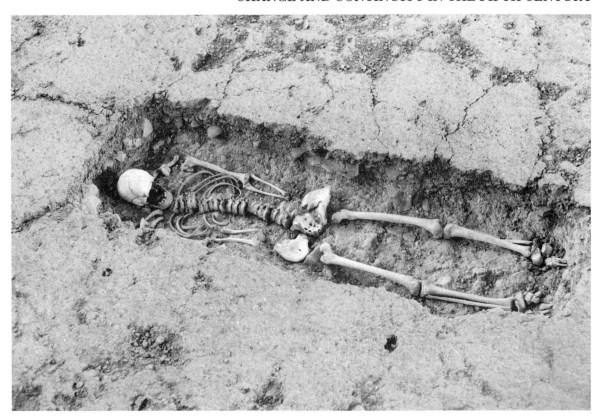

112 *Post-Roman inhumation grave at Fishbourne (West Sussex). Several graves were found, cut into the ruined building at a date unknown, but probably during the fifth century.*

similar material. Although we can do no more than speculate it is tempting to see such places as the refuges of groups of descendants of the more affluent and influential Romano-British who had managed to sustain some sort of connection with contacts in the ailing Roman Empire. The survival of some Latin words into Welsh is often quoted as evidence for a withdrawal of Romano-British Celtic culture towards the western part of Britain.

The ultimate fate of a romanized rural society in Britain is completely obscure. In the towns at least some sort of continuity is visible if only to the extent that many re-emerge in the sources as major settlements in succeeding centuries. For the rural settlements the connections are much vaguer. It is almost impossible for us to accept that a social and economic infrastructure which manifested itself in so many tangible ways could apparently disappear in the space of a few decades. But disap-

pear it did. This does not mean that people disappeared, merely that the means by which we are accustomed to identify their presence disappeared. This is difficult to come to terms with but what it may mean is that people found different ways to store wealth and express status during a time of stress and insecurity, ways which are not represented in the archaeological record.

It is extremely unlikely that there was any large-scale cessation of farming though there were probably localized changes such as the giving up of marginal land. Such pollen evidence as exists does not point to widespread reforestation. The nature of prevailing insecurity and its effect on the annual agricultural cycle is very difficult to gauge. The hopelessly inadequate and confusing (as well as confused) chroniclers, such as Gildas, paint pictures of wretched civilians plagued by famine and a constant barrage of violent and rapacious barbarians intent on wreaking maximum havoc and destruction well on into the fifth century. Gildas says the Britons either gave up and surrendered or took to the hills until resistance was organized under the leadership of the enigmatic Ambrosius Aurelianus which led to a period of peace. But Gildas was interested in making moral points rather than historical issues and we cannot take him at his word for details.

There has been an almost continuous academic debate over the chronology of the fifth century but the details are of little concern here. Even if we accept the basic truth of the above account it is unlikely that the violence was anything more than intermittent and very localized. 'Battles' and 'armies' are grand words but are more likely to have referred to skirmishes and armed bands. In other words agriculture and other basic rural activities are unlikely to have been profoundly affected. The emergence of the petty kings and chieftains of early Saxon England, complicated subsequently by the presence of the Church as a new player in the contest for wealth and property, shows that there were people to rule and farmland to control. Places like South Cadbury point to a residual component of society intent on preserving its connections with the classical world, which eventually faded, perhaps following small-scale emigrations to Gaul and the deaths of senior family members who would have clung to their memories more assiduously.

Nevertheless we cannot avoid the conclusion that there was a devastating cultural change in the way that the population of Britain organized and expressed themselves, recorded their affairs and stored their wealth. The fact that a Saxon church was built at Lullingstone makes it almost certain that the place's significance had been remembered. But as the house had long since fallen into ruin the memory was probably a dim one, carried down through generations of local families like a sepia photograph filled with half-forgotten relatives and other anonymous faces. The medieval church at Burford contains what appears to be a Romano-Celtic carved relief of Epona, a goddess of fertility. Half-hidden high up a wall it seems an incongruous element but it was obviously meant to be seen, if not too easily. In this way the Roman-ness of rural Britain became a curiosity, part venerated and part feared.

Where to visit the Roman countryside

Comparatively little of the buildings and settlements of the Romano-British countryside is visible today. Even so this is not an exhaustive catalogue by any means and is only intended to give details of the most impressive sites, as well as a reasonable cross-section. This means a heavy bias in favour of villas which are, for obvious reasons, confined to the central and southern part of Britain. Works listed under Further Reading include books which are comprehensive guides to visible remains of Roman Britain. Would-be visitors are advised to check in advance that sites are accessible, especially in the winter.

(Ordnance Survey grid references are shown in brackets)

Bignor, West Sussex (SU9814)
An exceptional villa site with a celebrated series of fourth-century mosaics. Most easily approached along minor roads from the A29 at Bury about 8km (5 miles) north of Arundel. Open daily during the summer season – from March to October inclusive. Closed Mondays March to May and October except on Bank Holidays.

Brading, Isle of Wight (SZ6086)
Like Bignor, Brading is famous for its fourth-century mosaics. Reached from Brading on the A3055 in the eastern part of the island between Ryde and Sandown. Open daily during the summer season between April and September inclusive.

Chedworth, Gloucestershire (SP0513)
Despite its glorious setting and size Chedworth is not the most absorbing villa site, though the entrance building now features a video presentation. Reached via Yanworth down a series of well-signposted minor roads off the A429 just south of Northleach where it crosses the A40.

Chysauster, Cornwall (SW4735)
Native stone-built village consisting of a number of houses. Reached from the B3311 which leaves the A30 just to the east of Penzance. Access daily from April to September inclusive.

Dolaucothi, Dyfed (SN6640)
Roman mines visible here along with later workings, but little to see. Accessed by minor roads from Pumpsaint on the A482 between Lampeter and Llandovery. Any time.

Fishbourne, West Sussex (SU8304)
One of the best-known of all Romano-British villas Fishbourne is an exceptionally large and early house. The north wing is the main visible part and is accompanied by a site museum. Signposted off the A27 at Fishbourne village just west of Chichester. Open daily March to November, Sundays only December to February.

Great Witcombe, Gloucestershire (SO8914)
Great Witcombe has the most outstanding setting of any visitable Romano-British villa though there is no custodian and consequently no on-site information or museum. Signposted up a minor road running south from the A417 between Cirencester and Gloucester about 8km (5 miles) east of the latter. Access at any reasonable time.

Littlecote, Wiltshire (SU2970)
Remains of the villa house and triconch hall

113 *The 'Dolphin' mosaic at Fishbourne (West Sussex). Second century.*

with re-laid Orpheus mosaic. Forms part of the Littlecote estate off the B4192 running west from Hungerford. Changes in ownership mean that at the time of writing (1992) there is no access to the Roman buildings, though this may change

Lullingstone, Kent (TQ5365)
Lullingstone's most famous finds, the busts and Christian paintings, are on display at the British Museum, but the site is a rewarding one with, exceptionally, almost the whole structure laid out under cover. Visitors have the use of a personal audio-cassette guide. Signposted from Eynsford on the A225 just south of the A20.

Lydney Park, Gloucestershire (SO6102)
The overgrown remains of the Temple of Nodens and other structures make an attractive visit but the site is privately owned and only accessible by prior appointment with the

Lydney Estate Office (Tel:0594-42844). Reached from the A48 between Gloucester and Chepstow.

Maiden Castle, Dorset (SY6688)
The remains of the Romano-Celtic temple lie in the north-east part of the sprawling Iron Age hillfort a short distance to the south-west of Dorchester, signposted off the A354. Access any time.

Newport, Isle of Wight (SZ5088)
Small winged-corridor house partially consolidated beneath a cover building in Avondale Road, Newport. Tessellated floors and hypocausts. Open daily during the summer season except Saturdays.

North Leigh, Oxfordshire (SP3915)
Courtyard villa almost entirely exposed but with little to see apart from wall footings and a mosaic. Signposted from the A4095 north-east of Witney, ignore the village which is some way from the villa. Access at any time.

Rockbourne, Hampshire (SU1217)
Now partly back-filled and with a modernized museum the villa lies in a secluded setting. Best approached by leaving the A338 at Fordingbridge up the B3078, and turning right at Sandleheath. Open from April to October but during the week closed in the mornings except in July and August.

South Cadbury, Somerset (ST6325)
Iron Age hillfort reoccupied and refortified in the fifth century by people sustaining connections with the classical world, though this is not evident from the present state of the ramparts. Reached from the A303 or A359 about 11km (7 miles) north-east of Yeovil.

Further reading

Although a great many sites have been excavated in the Romano-British countryside it is not always very easy to follow up the history and archaeology of an individual place. Excavations of a reasonably organized variety have been taking place since the nineteenth century but it is not unusual to find that publication was delayed for decades or more, and in fact may never have even taken place.

Most rural sites tend to be small scale and of more interest locally than nationally, so they are often published in the annual journal issued by the county archaeological society, for example *Archaeologia Cantiana* published annually by the Kent Archaeological Society. These are normally available for any particular county in the respective local libraries though university libraries will sometimes have a comprehensive set for the whole country. Sites with more significance, like Littlecote or Lullingstone, may be covered either in details or as a whole in the periodicals issued by national societies. For Roman Britain the most important is *Britannia*, published once a year by the Society for the Promotion of Roman Studies, 31–34 Gordon Square, London WC1H 0PP, though relevant articles also appear in the *Antiquaries Journal*, issued by the Society of Antiquaries in London. Easier to obtain than any of these is the bi-monthly magazine *Current Archaeology*, available on subscription from 9 Nassington Road, London NW3 2TX. This is a useful way of keeping in touch, with new sites often appearing in *Current Archaeology* long before anywhere else.

General reading

There are a number of histories of Roman Britain which are readily available. Most popular is S.S. Frere's *Britannia* now in its third edition (1987) and available in paperback. Other useful histories are Peter Salway's *Roman Britain* (1981) and Malcolm Todd's *Roman Britain (55BC–AD400)* (1981). For the latter part of the province's history A.S. Esmonde Cleary's *The Ending of Roman Britain* (1989) is an interesting analysis of the complex and contradictory evidence for the third and fourth centuries. For the Iron Age background Barry Cunliffe's *Iron Age Communities in Britain* has recently been revised in a third edition (1991).

For a synthesis of history and archaeology the recently published *Atlas of Roman Britain* (1990) by B. Jones and D. Mattingly covers an enormous amount of material with numerous maps and tables. Martin Millet's *The Romanization of Britain* (1990) is a very useful guide to current archaeological thinking on Roman Britain. Kevin Greene's *The Archaeology of the Roman Economy* (1986) is a useful introduction to modern understanding of the process of trade and production in the Roman world.

The countryside in general

There are relatively few books which cover rural Roman Britain in any great detail. One recent summary is R. Hingley's *Rural Settlement in Roman Britain* (1989) which is particularly concerned with looking at the different types of rural settlement which existed. A.L.F. Rivet's *Town and Country in Roman Britain* (1964), which has become a standard work, looked at the relationship between both aspects.

A small number of examples of country life and other incidents in this present book have been drawn from other periods, mainly from the seventeenth-century writings of Samuel Pepys (*Diary*, 15 July 1661), and John Evelyn (*Diary*, 27 September 1658, and the biography by John Bowle, 1981, p.239). The twentieth-century autobiography *Cider with Rosie*, by Laurie Lee, is also cited. The Tichborne Dole painting is most easily found in *A Social History of England* (1983) by Asa Briggs, p.146. Interesting accounts of drovers' roads from Wales into England used in the eighteenth and nineteenth centuries can be found in *The Drovers' Roads of Wales*, by S. Toulson (1977). With so little firm evidence for rural society in Roman Britain it is extremely important to be able to look carefully at recorded events and traditions from other periods. Parallels are rarely exact but the information gleaned can be extremely enlightening.

Villas

Villas have attracted more archaeological attention than any other aspect of the countryside. There are a number of books which cover the subject. J. Percival's *The Roman Villa. An Historical Introduction* (1976) puts the villa into its context as part of the Roman world. Surveys of Romano-British villas include: K. Branigan *The Roman Villa in South-West England* (1976), D.E. Johnston *Roman Villas* (Shire Archaeology 11, 1988), A.L.F. Rivet (Ed.) *The Roman Villa in Britain* (1969), M. Todd (Ed.) *Studies in the Romano-British Villa*. More recent papers appear in *The Economies of Romano-British Villas*, edited by K. Branigan and D. Miles (1988).

For the decoration of villas the reader should consult N. Davey and R. Ling *Wall-Painting in Roman Britain* (1982), R. Ling *Romano-British Wall-Painting* (Shire Archaeology 42, 1985), D.S. Neal *Roman Mosaics in Britain* (1981), and P. Johnson *Romano-British Mosaics* (Shire Archaeology 25, 1982).

Few specific villa sites have been published under a single title. Amongst the most interesting are: the Lullingstone villa which is published in two volumes (I – the Site, 1979, and II – the Finds, 1987) by the excavator Lt. Col. G.W. Meates for the Kent Archaeological Society; the Fishbourne Palace, also published in two volumes for site and finds (1971) as well as a single 'popular' volume in the Thames and

Hudson *New Aspects of Antiquity* series in the same year, by B.W. Cunliffe, and D. Miles' *Archaeology at Barton Court Farm, Abingdon, Oxon* (1984). The excavation of the remarkably well-preserved remains of the small villa at Redlands Farm, Stanwick, Northamptonshire, is described in *Current Archaeology*, no. 122, 1990, and various episodes in the long-term excavations at Piddington, Northamptonshire, also appear in the same magazine, in particular no. 117 (1989). For information about other sites the bibliography for Chapter 4 of the present author's *Buildings of Roman Britain* (1991) contains a detailed list in alphabetical order of site name.

Villages and other small settlements

Although the sites of numerous Romano-British villages are now known, extremely few have been excavated in any detail in modern times. One of these is Catsgore in Somerset, covered by Roger Leech's *Excavations at Catsgore, 1970–1973*, Bristol, 1982 and a further volume for 1979 excavations by Peter Ellis. Claydon Pike appears in *Current Archaeology* no. 86, 1983. Robin Hanley's *Villages in Roman Britain* (1987), no. 49, in the Shire Archaeology series looks at the subject more generally and includes plans of a number of different sites.

Religion

There are a number of general books about this subject which has always been popular in Romano-British studies. Martin Henig's *Religion in Roman Britain* (1984) covers most aspects, as does Graham Webster's *The British Celts and their Gods under Rome* (1986). For specific sites Lydney Park (1932), Maiden Castle (1943) and Nettleton (1982) have been published as monographs in the Research Reports series of the Society of Antiquaries of London by Mortimer Wheeler (Lydney and Maiden Castle) and W.J. Wedlake. Uley is the most recently published site, by A. Woodward and P. Leach. See the present author's *Buildings of Roman Britain* (1991), 249–250 for a bibliographical list of selected religious sites. However, most of the works referred to are generally only available in specialist libraries or university bookshops (if still in print).

Glossary

amphora The universal means of transporting perishables in the ancient world. There were many forms of this heavy pottery container, but almost all had handles and could be stacked against one another. The neck was usually plugged with wood and a painted inscription recorded the nature, quantity and owner of the contents.

axonometric Form of projection used to show buildings by drawing vertical lines directly from a plan. In this way proportions and relative dimensions are retained.

cella The inner chamber of a temple, where the cult statue was kept.

centuriated land Land divided up into regular units, usually rectangular. This allowed equally-sized plots to be awarded to military veterans and simplified administration for census and taxation purposes. In relatively undisturbed areas, for instance North Africa, large areas of these land divisions can be identified by aerial photography.

civitas A *civitas* was a community and in Roman Britain's case this meant a tribal community. The old tribal areas were used as the political sub-divisions of the province and each was ruled from its *civitas* capital, for example Cirencester, *Corinium Dobunnorum* 'Corinium [capital] of the Dobunni'.

colonia A city with special status as a community of full Roman citizens. In Roman Britain's case all certain *coloniae* had been established on the sites of former legionary fortresses, for example Colchester.

flue-tile A special hollow rectangular tile which was used to build channels for carrying hot air through walls as part of a hypocaust central-heating system.

isometric Form of projection similar to **axonometric** but the plan has its angles altered to create an illusion of perspective.

mortarium Hemispherical pottery mixing-bowl with a pronounced lip and spout. Normally made from a coarse ware with gritting to aid grinding.

nymphaeum Shrine dedicated to nymphs, female spirits often associated with water or woods.

oppidum Latin word for a town. Used by ancient authors like Caesar to refer to the large low-lying native settlements in northern Britain and Gaul.

samian A fine red-slip type of pottery imported from Gaul during the first, second and early third centuries. There were many forms, most of them plain but some were decorated in moulds or by other processes.

siliqua Modern term for the smallest silver coins issued during the fourth century. Normally of good quality metal but erratically issued.

tesserae The small stones used to make up mosaic floors by laying them in a prepared and marked out mortar bed. Sources include old brick and samian pottery for red stones, limestone for white, and shale for black. An average sized floor could easily contain over 150,000 of them.

tria nomina Formal name with three components: the *praenomen* 'forename', the *nomen* 'family name', and the *cognomen* 'personal name', normally indicative of citizenship.

villa Latin word for a house or farm, usually qualified, for example *villa rustica* 'country house/farm' or *villa urbana*. The word is normally used in a rural context but in modern parlance is commonly used for any Roman house found outside towns regardless of whether it was connected with farming or not.

vicus Small settlement or town of low status.

Index

INDEX

General Index